Religious Studies
FOR COMMON ENTRANCE

13+

Exam Practice Answers

Religious Studies

FOR COMMON ENTRANCE

13+

Exam Practice Answers

**Susan Grenfell and
Michael Wilcockson**

GALORE
PARK

AN HACHETTE UK COMPANY

About the authors

Susan Grenfell has taught Religious Studies to Common Entrance and Scholarship level for eighteen years, ten of them as Head of Department at St Hugh's School, Faringdon. She is author of the textbook *Religious Studies for Common Entrance* and has led seminars on teaching RS at IAPS and ISRSA conferences.

Michael Wilcockson was brought up in Cambridge and studied Theology at Balliol College, Oxford. After completing his PGCE at Pembroke College, Cambridge he became Head of Divinity at Aldenham School and later at The Leys School, Cambridge. He was appointed Head of Divinity at Eton College in 1996 and in 2010 became the college's first Head of Philosophy. He was a Farmington Fellow at Harries Manchester College, Oxford in 2003 and Visiting Scholar at Pembroke College, Cambridge in 2010. He is Chief Examiner for A Level Religious Studies for a large examination board and Chief Setter for Common Entrance Religious Studies for ISEB. He is author of many textbooks for Common Entrance, GCSE and A Level. He is a Fellow of the Chartered Institute of Educational Assessors.

Every effort has been made to trace all copyright holders, but if any have been inadvertently overlooked the publishers will be pleased to make the necessary arrangements at the first opportunity.

Hachette UK's policy is to use papers that are natural, renewable and recyclable products and made from wood grown in sustainable forests. The logging and manufacturing processes are expected to conform to the environmental regulations of the country of origin.

Orders: please contact Bookpoint Ltd, 130 Milton Park, Abingdon, Oxon OX14 4SB. Telephone: (44) 01235 827720. Fax: (44) 01235 400454. Email education@bookpoint.co.uk. Lines are open from 9 a.m. to 5 p.m., Monday to Saturday, with a 24-hour message answering service. Visit our website at www.galorepark.co.uk for details of other revision guides for Common Entrance, examination papers and Galore Park publications.

ISBN: 978 1 471853 40 1

© Susan Grenfell and Michael Wilcockson 2015

First published in 2015 by

Galore Park Publishing Ltd,

An Hachette UK Company

Carmelite House

50 Victoria Embankment

London EC4Y 0DZ

www.galorepark.co.uk

Impression number   10 9 8 7 6 5 4 3 2

Year   2019 2018 2017

Typeset in India

Printed in the UK

A catalogue record for this title is available from the British Library.

Contents

Introduction

This book gives examples of possible answers to the questions set in *Religious Studies for Common Entrance 13+ Exam Practice Questions*.

Chapters 1 and 2 provide answers to the Bible text questions from Sections 1 and 2 of the exam. Chapters 3–9 provide answers to the 'World Religions and Contemporary Issues' questions from Section 3 of the exam.

Answers

The answers given in this book are not intended to be definitive as there are, of course, many ways in which a question might be answered to gain high marks.

Sections 1 and 2

The **Part a** and **b questions** are straightforward so, although the wording may vary slightly, answers should contain approximately the same information as those in this book.

The **Part c questions** are more complex so answers may vary more significantly. Different points may be chosen and they may be explained in a different way. If an answer is very different from the one in this book, look back at the *Religious Studies for Common Entrance 13+ Revision Guide* or another reliable textbook to determine whether a mistake has been made.

A useful format for answering this type of question is to make a **statement** that answers the question; then support it with **evidence** from the text. For example:

Question: What does the story of Cain and Abel teach about sin?

Answer: *The story teaches that sin begins in the mind* [statement]. *God rejected Cain's offering because he had anger in his heart* [evidence]. *One sin can lead to another* [statement]. *Cain lied to God about Abel's whereabouts* [evidence]. *Sin has consequences* [statement]. *Cain was sent out from the farm and lived the life of a nomad* [evidence].

There are many ways to approach **Part d questions** and often there are no right or wrong answers. You may find that you don't agree with the arguments in some of the answers in this book. That is to be expected as we all hold different views. These answers are designed to show how different points of view can be argued. Some take a traditional approach and others have a more liberal interpretation. What matters is that clear *reasons* are given for the answer.

Here are two completely different answers to the same Part d question. Both are equally right.

Question: 'The Burning Bush is the most important moment in the Old Testament.' Do you agree? Give reasons to support your answer.

Answer 1:

If Moses had not returned to Egypt and brought the Israelites out, they would not have wandered in the desert and come to Mount Sinai. God would not have given Moses the Law and they would not have established themselves in Israel. Their whole history would have been different and even Jesus might not have been born. Therefore it is the most important moment, not just in the Old Testament, but arguably in the history of Judaism and Christianity.

On the other hand, you could pick any of the moments when God intervened in the lives of His people and say the same thing. Also, if God is all powerful, He would have found another way of rescuing the Israelites if Moses had refused to go.

I think that it is difficult to single out any one event as being the most important and it would also limit the power of God to do so. Therefore I disagree with the statement.

Answer 2:

This story can be seen as the most important moment in the Old Testament because it is the moment when God revealed who He was in a way He had not done before. By saying that Moses was to tell the Israelites that 'I AM has sent you', God revealed Himself not only as the creator God but as a God of justice who saves His people. This aspect of God's nature is a major recurring theme of the Bible.

On the other hand, there are other arguably more important moments in the Old Testament. For example, when God made His covenant with Abraham, He established His unique relationship with the Jewish people. By the time of the Israelites' slavery in Egypt, God was already committed to helping them.

Therefore, at the Burning Bush God reveals so much more of who He is than anywhere else in the Old Testament and that is why this story is more important than any other.

The important point is that whatever is written must be supported with evidence. Examples from the text and knowledge of the background history and theology should be included. Unsupported statements will not gain marks.

Section 3

Some topics in Section 3 contain more information than there is space or time to include in an answer. Answers may therefore not exactly match those in the book. This does not matter as long as the key pieces of information are included. The important thing is not to write about details and miss out the main facts.

Answer length

In Sections 1 and 2 your answers should be approximately of the following length:

- **Part a:** A few words
- **Part b:** 60–80 words
- **Part c:** 60–80 words
- **Part d:** 150–180 words.

In Section 3 your answers should be approximately 60–80 words long. The answers in this book have kept to these length guidelines.

Assessment criteria

The assessment criteria tell the examiner what to look for in an answer. These criteria can therefore be used to give marks (and levels) to practice answers. The assessment criteria are arranged according to the Assessment Objective (AO) covered by each type of question. The Assessment Objectives are knowledge (AO1), understanding (AO2) and evaluation (AO3).

AO1: Knowledge
Sections 1 and 2 (Part a)

Level	Mark	Level Descriptor
1–2	1	Gives one simple piece of relevant information.
3–4	2	Gives two correct and appropriately detailed pieces of knowledge.

Sections 1 and 2 (Part b) and Section 3

Level	Mark	Level Descriptor
1	1	Gives a **very poor** answer: an isolated example of a simple piece of relevant information.
2	2	Gives a **basic** answer: limited knowledge of a relevant idea presented in a structured way.
3	3	Gives a **broadly satisfactory** answer: a description presented in a structured way but lacking precision and some knowledge; moderate use of English.
4	4	Gives a **satisfactory** answer: a description showing more precise knowledge and understanding.
5	5	Gives a **good** answer: a precise description summarising significant details; a high level of knowledge and understanding.
6	6	Gives a **very good** answer: a coherent and precise description; an incisive summary of the significant details; very good command of English.

AO2: Understanding
Sections 1 and 2 (Part c)

Level	Mark	Level Descriptor
1	1	Gives a **very poor** answer: an isolated example of a simple piece of relevant information.
2	2	Gives a **basic** answer: a limited understanding of a relevant idea.
3	3	Gives a **broadly satisfactory** answer: an explanation presented in a structured way but lacking detail and some knowledge; moderate use of English.
4	4	Gives a **satisfactory** answer: an explanation of more than one idea presented with some detail and understanding.
5	5	Gives a **good** answer: a detailed explanation of several ideas with a good level of knowledge and understanding.
6	6	Gives a **very good** answer: a coherent and comprehensive explanation of several ideas (with sound reference to background, history, other relevant passages, etc.); very good command of English.

AO3: Evaluation
Sections 1 and 2 (Part d)

Level	Mark	Level Descriptor
1	1	Gives a **very poor** answer: no essay structure; a very brief answer; a statement with no reasoning; very little reference to the question; poor or irrelevant examples; makes little sense.
2	2	Gives a **basic** answer: a viewpoint is expressed with minimum justification; an example given; limited relevance.
3	3	Gives a **broadly satisfactory** answer: some structure or organisation of ideas; lack of clear reasoning; some relevant points; unbalanced; limited examples.
4	4	Gives a **satisfactory** answer: reasonably clear structure and balanced answer; some examples and sound explanation; reasonable expression; one or two relevant points made; another point of view considered, supported by reasons.
5	5	Gives a **good** answer: good, clear structure and balanced answer; well-chosen examples with a sound grasp of their meaning; sound assessment of ideas; another point of view considered, supported by good reasons.
6	6	Gives a **very good** answer: very good structure; ideas developed in a balanced way; well-chosen and relevant examples; another point of view considered, supported by clear reasons.
7	7	Gives an **excellent** answer: excellent structure and balanced answer; very good use of language; focuses on the question; well-chosen examples to illustrate the points being made; another point of view considered, supported by very clear reasoning.

Marking Part d questions

Part d questions are marked using the AO3 Evaluation assessment criteria shown above. The marks will also depend, however, on the standard each senior school sets.

The following examples show how the marking scheme has been applied to some actual Common Entrance answers written under examination conditions.

Level 7 answer

Question: 'In Jesus' parable of the Lost Son the real lessons are to be learned from the behaviour of the elder son.' Do you agree? Give reasons to support your answer.

Answer	Comments
I agree to an extent with this statement because in this parable the elder son is jealous of his brother and angry with his father. He can't understand why his brother is forgiven so easily. As Jesus said to the high priests a doctor is needed for the ill not for those who are well. So this parable shows you how not to react if you aren't being rewarded or helped by God.	It is probably not a good idea to agree or disagree so early. You could be a bit more objective and say, 'There are good reasons why the question is right because the elder son is jealous...'

This is a good piece of cross-referencing to Jesus' teaching to support this bit of the argument. Notice the use of 'so' to link the example to the argument the candidate is making. |
| So there are lessons to be learned from the elder son. It shows you that you should be pleased when someone repents. | Strictly this is not a new paragraph but it reinforces the candidate's support for the view expressed in the question. |
| On the other hand I don't think the real reason lessons learned are from the elder son's behaviour. Surely the lesson to learn is that however much you have sinned God will be there for you when you repent. It shows that however low you go (the son ate with the pigs which is a great sin in Judaism), God will forgive you and give you a clean slate. | The use of 'on the other hand...' is a neat way of showing the weaknesses of the argument stated so far and presents another view.

The alternative view is expressed clearly and with a brief reference to the parable. |
| In conclusion the main purpose of this parable is to illustrate the generous forgiveness of God. So, in fact, the real lessons are learned from the behaviour of the father – just as Jesus also taught in the parable of the lost sheep. | The conclusion makes sure that the question is referred to and answered.

Technically the conclusion, which disagrees with the statement, contradicts the opening sentence where the candidate agreed with the statement. This might lose the candidate a mark. But the examiner has been generous here!

Another reference to Jesus' teaching reinforces the candidate's argument. |
| | **7/7 marks** |

Level 4 answer

Question: 'Miracles do not happen today.' Do you agree? Give reasons to support your answer.

Answer	Comments
Yes, miracles do happen today but nowadays many scientists try to prove that it wasn't a miracle and lead everyone into having no faith. Miracles tend to happen every so often but when they do, they are quite extraordinary. For example, when someone is in hospital and suffering from an incurable disease, like MS, they are suddenly healed and the only logical explanation is from an act of God. This, once again, shows us that God loves us and that we are all in one community together. God cares about us and helps us all the time.	This answer would be immediately improved if each part of the argument were given a new paragraph.

It is never a good idea to start by saying 'yes' or 'no'. This makes the answer too chatty. In this case, a brief definition of a miracle would then make the next stage of the argument clear.

There is some confusion here. How can some miracles be ordinary and some extraordinary! A miracle is usually defined as an extraordinary event.

The example is good but to make use of it the candidate also needs to discuss why logically it might not be an act of God.

The conclusion is irrelevant, even if it is true. |
| | **4/7 marks** |

Level 2 answer

Question: 'The Creation accounts in the Bible give us no guidance about how to live our lives today.' Do you agree? Give reasons for your answer.

Answer	Comments
This quote is untrue as it does give us useful and moral guidance as to how to live today. It teaches us to carry out instructions or it can lead to consequences. It also gives us an aspect of what is right and what is wrong. It may be just a story with little meaning but it does keep to what we have been told and tells us that we should keep to the law and modern day rules. Lack of these simple things very often leads to punishments as it did in the story. All of these are from the story and provide useful guidance for all of us today.	Even if this answer were divided into paragraphs, it has no structure and is so vague that paragraphs would not improve it. This shows what happens when there has been no attempt to plan an answer. This is a promising start. This makes very little sense and at the very least needs an example from the Bible to clarify the point being made, for example the actions of Adam and Eve in Eden and punishments by God. There is no indication what these 'simple things' are. This is a kind of conclusion but as there is no argument it is almost worthless. **2/7 marks**

Interpreting the Old Testament

Theme 1: God, human nature and covenant

1.1 The Creation

Part a questions:

1   The Sabbath is the Jewish day of rest.   (2)

2   Stewardship is looking after the world for God.   (2)

3   The Garden of Eden is the garden in Genesis 2 where everything is perfect.   (2)

4   The earth was formless and empty before God began creation.   (2)

5   God formed Adam from the dust and breathed life into his nostrils.   (2)

Part b questions:

1   God planted a garden and called it Eden. In the middle of it He planted two trees. One
    tree was the tree of life and the other was the tree of knowledge of good and evil. Four
    rivers flowed out of Eden. God placed Adam in the garden and told him to look after it and
    eat from all the trees, but he told him not to eat from the tree of knowledge. Later God
    created a helper for Adam called Eve.   (6)

2   On the first four days of creation God created everything except living creatures. He
    created light and darkness, calling them day and night. Then He made sea and dry land
    and created vegetation to grow on the land. This produced plants, seeds, trees and fruit.
    On the fourth day He created the sun, moon and stars and everything was good.   (6)

3   God commanded that the sea should be filled with living creatures like fish and the
    great sea monsters. On the sixth day He created large and small animals, both domestic
    and wild. At the end He created human beings in his own image to rule over everything
    He had created.   (6)

4   God created man first by forming him from the dust of the earth. Then He breathed
    into his nostrils and he began to live. Later God put man into a deep sleep. While he was
    asleep God took one of his ribs and then healed the wound. From the rib He created
    woman. So man had a companion and helper.   (6)

5   The Garden of Eden contained everything that human beings need for life and included
    some luxuries such as precious stones and metals. Four rivers ran through the land to water
    it and God planted trees. Two particular trees were the tree of life and the tree of the
    knowledge of good and evil. Man, animals and birds occupied the land.   (6)

Part c questions:

1   God was pleased with His creation for three reasons. Firstly, because everything was created
    in its right place and therefore could sustain life. Without light, life would not be possible
    and without sea and dry land, animal and plant life would cease. Plants and animals need

each other to survive. Secondly, it was good because the universe is beautiful; modern science constantly reveals this. Thirdly, it is pleasing because, being created in God's image, humans are intelligent and can carry on God's work. (6)

2 God gave human beings two instructions: to have children and to rule over all creatures on earth. The first is significant because God intended that they should populate the earth. The second instruction is important because they were made in God's image, having the power to care for the environment and wildlife as God himself would care and be stewards of the earth. (6)

3 The story of the Garden of Eden teaches that God is powerful. He created everything in the Garden. The story also shows that He expects obedience from human beings; He commanded them not to eat from the two trees in the centre. God is portrayed as a listening and loving God who was fully aware of Adam not having a suitable companion and responded to this need. (6)

4 Genesis 2 teaches that human beings need each other. God gave Adam a companion and they lived together. It also teaches us that humans are inventive. Adam named all the animals and birds. The story shows that humans need a sense of purpose. God put Adam into the Garden to work the land and take care of it. The last thing it teaches about humans is that in the beginning they were without sin. It says they were 'naked but without shame'. (6)

5 Genesis 1 teaches that humans were to rule over all living creatures and that God gave both humans and animals plants and seeds as food. This implies that animals and birds were not to be eaten. Genesis 2 shows a close relationship between humans and animals when Adam names them all. God created animals to be companions for Adam. (6)

Part d questions:

1 Modern science does contradict Genesis 1 if it is read in a fairly literal way. For example, there is no mention of the Big Bang in Genesis. Modern views of evolution suggest that matter and life were created over a very long time and not in the six days Genesis describes. Humans were not created at the beginning but evolved from lower life forms.

On the other hand, if Genesis 1 is a theological story then it is telling us that the universe is not here by chance and is ordered so that it can support life. Many modern scientists support this because there are ways in which the universe seems to be 'fine-tuned' to support life, such as the rate at which the universe expanded after the Big Bang.

I think that modern science has disproved Genesis 1 as a factual story but it does not necessarily disprove its theological meaning. (7)

2 Environmental problems such as global warming, pollution and the destruction of animal habitats cause many people to say this statement is true. Unless something is done quickly and human beings start taking their stewardship responsibilities seriously, life on earth will change for ever. Some scientists say that icebergs melting into the Gulf Stream could lead to another ice age.

On the other hand, looking after the world has always been important. God commanded the first humans to care for the land and protect wildlife. It was as important a hundred years ago as it is now. Perhaps if our ancestors had not caused so much pollution during the Industrial Revolution, we would not have the problems we have now. People have always had to balance their needs against the good of the earth.

Unfortunately, human greed has led to climate change and major environmental catastrophes so I agree with the statement. It is more important now than ever before. (7)

3 Some people might argue that because God gives humans many chances to make things right again, perhaps the world could be perfect. Environmental groups such as A Rocha are working hard to restore land that has been spoiled and to give animals and birds places to live and rear their young. Governments are concerned with reducing pollution and industry is trying to be 'greener'.

On the other hand, we have got so used to how we live now that to try to turn the clock back would be impossible. Humans are too greedy to work together on a grand scale, even if a few groups manage it. Christians argue too that since the Fall, sin has entered the world and it can never be perfect again.

It would be nice to feel that we could make everything new and perfect as it once was, but we are too selfish and things have gone too far. Therefore I agree with the statement that the world can never again be perfect. (7)

4 Some people would argue that the statement is wrong because Genesis 2 says that woman was created out of man, which would make them essentially the same. Adam said of Eve, 'This is now bone of my bones and flesh of my flesh'. If Eve were to be Adam's helper that meant that they shared in the same work of looking after the land. They were also both without sin.

However, Adam was made out of dust and God breathed life into his nostrils. Eve was made from Adam's rib and brought to him for approval; God did not breathe in to her. This suggests that women are different. Also, the woman has to leave her family and be united with the man, which is different too.

On the whole, I don't think that Genesis 2 is making a statement about differences between men and women but about how they relate to each other. Therefore I disagree with the statement. (7)

5 Some Christians (called creationists) believe that every word in Genesis 1 and 2 is true and that they were intended to be an account of how God created the world. They argue that the order of events closely follows the order that things happened in the beginning and they claim it all happened about six thousand years ago.

Other Christians believe that the stories were intended as parables. These parables reveal the deeper truth that however the world came together, it was God who breathed life into it and was the creative force behind it. The language is symbolic and not supposed to be taken literally. For example, when Eve was created from Adam's rib it showed equality between the sexes.

On balance, I agree with the statement. It is difficult to think that the stories were intended to be taken literally although they speak to people of God's power and authority. (7)

1.2 The Garden of Eden and the Fall

Part a questions:

1 The Fall is the moment when Adam and Eve fell from grace and disobeyed God. (2)

2 Sin is disobeying God and separating oneself from Him. (2)

3 Temptation is the desire to do something wrong. (2)

4 God punished the serpent by making him crawl on his belly. (2)

5 The Garden of Eden is the garden in Genesis 2 where everything is perfect. (2)

Part b questions:

1 The serpent tempted the woman to eat the fruit from the tree of the knowledge of good and evil, which God had forbidden the man and woman to eat. It told her that she would not die but would be like God, knowing what was good and bad. The woman decided the fruit looked delicious and that she would like to be wise, so she ate some. Then she gave some to the man. When they had both eaten, they realised they were naked. They made coverings from fig leaves and hid from God when He called. (6)

2 The serpent was the tempter because he asked the woman if God had really told her not to eat from any tree in the garden. When the woman explained that it was only the fruit from the tree in the middle of the garden that they could not eat, he said she would not really die if she ate it. Instead her eyes would be opened and she would be like God, knowing good and evil. (6)

3 God walked in the Garden and called to the man and the woman, who were hiding. They told God they were ashamed because they were naked. When God learned that they had eaten the forbidden fruit, He asked who was responsible. The man blamed the woman and she blamed the serpent. God cursed the serpent. Then He punished the man and the woman and sent them out from the Garden. However, He also made them clothes from animal skins. (6)

4 The serpent had to crawl on its belly and eat dust for all its life. God put hostility between the offspring of the serpent and the children of the woman. They would crush the serpent's head and it would bite their heel. The woman would have greater pain in child-bearing and would be ruled over by the man. The man would have to work hard to make the ground grow food. He now knew that he would die and return to dust. They were also banished from the garden. (6)

5 The serpent tempted Eve to eat the fruit from the tree of knowledge. She did so and gave some to Adam. After they had eaten they knew they were naked so they hid from God. God was angry when He learned what had happened and punished the serpent and Adam and Eve. They were no longer allowed to live in the Garden and would have to work hard to produce food. They both realised they were mortal. (6)

Part c questions:

1 The most significant thing about the punishments was that human relationships changed with each other, with nature and with God. They showed that men and women would no longer be equal. Humans would struggle with nature and making the earth grow things. Pain would be part of their experience. The serpent's punishment meant that humans would continually battle against evil. This battle would take place in their consciences and in their fight against natural evil in the world. (6)

2 The story of the Fall has several things to teach about human nature. Firstly, humans are easily led astray. The serpent only had to tell Eve that she wouldn't die but would become wise like God and she gave in. Secondly, humans will always try to shift the blame onto someone else as Adam and Eve did. Thirdly, humans can feel shame when they do something wrong, and lastly, they are greedy and ambitious. Adam and Eve wanted to be like God. (6)

3 The story of the Fall teaches that God is holy. He cannot allow sin near him, which is why he expelled Adam and Eve from the Garden. It shows that God will judge behaviour and punish wrong-doing just as He punished Adam and Eve. However, God is also merciful because He made clothes for them. It shows God's power that He only had to say something would happen for it to take place. (6)

4 God is holy and cannot have sin near him. Adam and Eve cut themselves off from God by sinning and disobeying him, so He expelled them from the Garden. He also had to protect the way to the Tree of Life. God could no longer trust them to obey Him. They had already eaten the fruit from one of the forbidden trees. Human beings had to learn how to be reconciled with God by leading lives pleasing to Him before they could approach Him again. (6)

5 The Tree of Knowledge is significant because of the fruit on it. To eat the fruit was to know both good and evil, whereas before Adam and Eve had only known good. It was significant because it was forbidden and so when they ate the fruit, they were disobeying God. Instead of trusting God to look after them, they wanted to develop their own set of values and survive without Him. (6)

Part d questions:

1 Some people would say the greatest evil today is racism because it works so obviously against the Christian principles of justice and love. We all share the horror of racist crimes such as the holocaust and apartheid in South Africa. Because world peace depends on the ability to live together in harmony, racism must be rooted out before anything else can be achieved.

On the other hand, bad as racism is, greed could be a greater evil. Racism only continues because of it. Greed is entirely selfish and causes injustice and poverty on a global scale. This can be seen in the actions of some multi-national corporations. Their actions may not be particularly racist but they work against everyone who stands in their way. Greed is one of the seven deadly sins for good reason.

In conclusion, I think that although racism is unacceptable, greed is worse because it has wider and often more lasting consequences. (7)

2 Some people would say that all wrong-doing should be punished because that is the way you learn the difference between right and wrong. For example, a child might be punished for taking a biscuit from the tin without asking. Punishment is a deterrent and if you know that you will always be punished you are less likely to do wrong.

Other people might argue that some wrong-doing is more complicated. For example, you might break the speed limit because you need to get a very sick person to hospital. They might also argue that just as Jesus showed mercy to 'sinners', so on occasion should we. Sometimes a loving response that explains why a certain action is wrong is far more effective than a punishment.

On balance, although something like speeding is always wrong in the same way as stealing is, there are times when punishment is the wrong response. Therefore I disagree with the statement. (7)

3 Most people would agree with this statement because we all want good things for ourselves. Adam and Eve were greedy for the forbidden fruit, and thousands of years on people's actions are still governed by self-interest. Children have to learn to share because they would naturally want to keep everything for themselves. Our advertising industry plays on our greed for material things.

On the other hand, there are plenty of people in the world whose lives are spent in service to others. Mother Teresa did not think of her own interests when she helped the poor in Calcutta. Neither did Jackie Pullinger consider her own comfort when she worked with drug addicts in Hong Kong.

In conclusion, I think that although we are all naturally selfish and greedy it is possible to overcome these instincts. (7)

4 Telling the truth is part of honesty and integrity, therefore it is very important. Our system of justice depends on everyone telling the truth. Relationships between people are based on trust so there is an expectation that everyone should always tell the truth.

On the other hand, there are times when telling the truth would be harmful. Government leaders, for example, sometimes have to withhold information or deliberately lie. This might be to control a situation where the truth would lead to panic and endanger lives. Spies have to lead a life of deceit to work for their country. Even in ordinary life, telling the truth might hurt someone so we tell a small lie.

So, although it might seem that telling the truth is something everyone should do, there are clearly times when it is sensible not to tell the whole truth and even to tell a lie. (7)

5 The story of the Fall raises many issues. It is about actions, consequences and responsibility. If we disobey the rules we are likely to be punished. Like Adam and Eve, we have freedom of choice but we have to take responsibility for our actions. In these respects, the lessons learned are as relevant to non-religious people as they are to religious people.

On the other hand, some might say that the message of the Fall is only a religious one. It is about how sin entered the world. It explains how the relationship between human beings and God was broken. It also offers an explanation for suffering. If you don't believe in God the lessons in the story will be irrelevant.

Although the Fall offers a religious explanation for suffering, the lessons about human nature have something to teach everyone. You cannot behave exactly as you wish without suffering the consequences. (7)

1.3 Cain and Abel

Part a questions:

1 Justice is treating others fairly. (2)

2 Cain and Abel were the sons of Adam and Eve. Cain was a farmer and Abel was a shepherd. (2)

3 Sacrifice is giving up something for something of greater value. (2)

4 Abel offered the best lamb in his flock as a sacrifice. (2)

5 Sin is disobeying God and separating oneself from Him. (2)

Part b questions:

1 God rejected Cain's offering, which made Cain very angry as his brother's offering was accepted. God told him that if he had done the right things he would be smiling but sin was crouching at his door ready to devour him. Cain was so angry that he killed his brother. God punished Cain by sending him out to be a restless wanderer. He put a mark on him to protect him from other tribes who might kill him. (6)

2 Cain and Abel both offered sacrifices to God. Abel offered the fat portions of his firstborn lambs and Cain offered some of his crop. God accepted Abel's offering but rejected Cain's. He said that if Cain did what was right his sacrifice would also be acceptable. God said that sin was crouching at his door ready to pounce. Cain was so jealous of Abel that he killed him. (6)

3 God asked him where Abel was. Cain said he was not his brother's keeper but God said that Abel's blood was crying out for justice. God said that Cain would be under a curse and the ground would no longer produce crops for him. Cain would become a nomad. Cain was afraid

that the people would kill him so God put a protective mark on him, saying that anyone who harmed him would suffer seven times as much. (6)

4 In the first conversation God asked Cain why he was so angry. He said that if he did what was right he would be accepted. Sin was crouching at his door but Cain must control it. In the second conversation God asked where Abel was. Cain said that he was not his brother's keeper. God said Abel's blood was crying out and because of what he had done Cain was under a curse. Cain would wander the earth and to protect him from being killed God said He would put a mark on him. (6)

5 Cain and Abel both offered sacrifices to God but Cain's was rejected. God said it was because he did not do what was right. Cain was so angry that he killed Abel. When God found out He banished Cain, making him wander the earth. The ground would not produce crops for him. Cain was so frightened of the other tribes that God put a protective mark on him. (6)

Part c questions:

1 The story teaches that God knows what is in people's hearts. He knew Cain was angry and jealous. It shows that God cares about justice. He heard Abel's blood 'crying out from the ground' and acted. God is shown to punish wrong-doing as He punished Cain by banishing him. However God is also merciful because He gave Cain a second chance and protected him with his mark. (6)

2 The main reason Cain murdered Abel was that he was jealous of his good relationship with God. God had accepted Abel's sacrifice but not his. This made Cain angry, and he did not listen to God's advice or warning about sin and how it was waiting to consume him. He did not change his attitude nor try to control his anger. Instead he looked for an opportunity to kill Abel. (6)

3 Cain's sacrifice was rejected because he sinned. We know this because God told him that if he did what was right his offering would be accepted. His attitude was also wrong because he could not control his temper or his actions. God said sin was crouching at his door. Lastly there is no mention of the quality of the produce Cain offered, unlike the description of Abel's as being the best, and he may have selected random or inferior items. (6)

4 Firstly, the story of Cain and Abel teaches us that human beings want to be close to God and accepted by Him. Abel wanted to offer the best of his flock. Secondly, it teaches that human nature is weak. Cain gave in very easily to his feelings against Abel. Thirdly, it teaches that people want to be better than others. Cain was jealous of his brother's righteousness. (6)

5 The story teaches that sin is part of our nature. God told Cain it was crouching at his door and wanted to control him. It teaches that anger is sinful because it gets in the way of a right relationship with God. Cain's sacrifice was refused because of his actions and his attitude. It teaches that anger can lead to sin. Cain went out and deliberately killed his brother. (6)

Part d questions:

1 Human beings feel anger and jealousy at times. Sometimes it leads them to do bad things. Jealous husbands kill their wives and jealous brothers hurt younger brothers if they think their parents are treating them unfairly. Many people would say that it takes a special kind of person to be gentle like Abel. So, in this respect, we may be more like Cain than Abel.

On the other hand, there are plenty of times when we do the right thing and even go out of our way to help people. Many people go to church and pray as Abel must have prayed, and try to lead good lives. One example is Mother Teresa, who offered herself as a sacrifice to God when she served him in India among the poor.

I think that although we all have a temper, it is not true that we are more like Cain, who was a murderer and a liar. We are probably a mixture of the two. (7)

2 In many ways this is true. People are far too busy with their lives to think of others. The media is always reminding them that they deserve the good things they have. This feeling of having worked hard for themselves makes many people think that they do not have to help anyone else.

On the other hand, most people make sacrifices, even if it is only for their families. There are also many people who make far bigger sacrifices to help others. Mother Teresa gave up her life to help the poor in India. Charities such as Christian Aid can only function because people are willing to sacrifice time and money.

Therefore I disagree with the statement, although it is true that we are all naturally selfish. However, most of us overcome this and give up time and resources to make life better for others. (7)

3 Many people say capital punishment is the only way to be sure someone won't kill again. It also acts as a deterrent to others. Executing a murderer shows the world that justice has been done. If you take someone's life, then yours should be taken. The Bible justifies this law by saying 'an eye for an eye and a tooth for a tooth'.

On the other hand, Jesus taught that we should love our enemies and do good to those who mistreat us. To execute someone makes us as bad as the murderer. Crime figures also show that capital punishment does not work as a deterrent. Lastly, innocent people can be executed. For example, Timothy Evans was hanged in 1950 for a murder that his lodger committed.

On balance, I disagree with the statement. Society is better off without capital punishment; in prison there is always hope that a person might change. (7)

4 It is difficult to know what really motivates us to do things. Even good things can be done for selfish reasons. We wash the car for our parents because we secretly hope they will take us to the cinema. Giving money to charity makes us feel good about ourselves. Those who work for the people in poor countries do so because it makes them feel fulfilled.

However, to say that no one acts with pure motives is harsh. Dietrich Bonhoeffer left a life of safety in America to help his fellow countrymen in Germany even though he knew it meant almost certain death. Oscar Romero fought against injustice in San Salvador although he knew it would put his life in danger.

I think that the statement is probably true. We do good things for all kinds of reasons and doing something purely out of love or concern for another is rare. (7)

5 The doctrine of 'original sin' says that we are all sinful because of the Fall. Adam and Eve disobeyed God and so brought sin into the world. If one takes this line then it might well be true to say that it was his parents' fault that Cain killed Abel. Many people today argue that they were not responsible for their actions because they had a terrible upbringing.

On the other hand, even if the first man and woman sinned, everyone has a choice as to whether or not to do something bad. Cain alone had the choice whether to kill Abel or not, so the decision to murder had nothing to do with his parents. We all have moral responsibility whatever background we come from.

Therefore, I disagree with the statement. It was Cain's fault that he sinned even though it was his parents' fault that sin came into the world. (7)

1.4 The near sacrifice of Isaac

Part a questions:

1 Sacrifice is giving up something for something of greater value. (2)

2 Abraham was the founder of the Jewish people and the father of Isaac. (2)

3 A covenant is an agreement between God and His people. (2)

4 Faith is having an active trust in God or a person. (2)

Part b questions:

1 God told Abraham to sacrifice Isaac so he took him to Mount Moriah and built an altar. He was about to kill Isaac when an angel told him to stop. He said that God had seen that he honoured and obeyed God. Abraham saw a ram and sacrificed that instead. The angel said that Abraham would have as many descendants as sand on the seashore and stars in the sky. They would conquer their enemies and through him all nations would be blessed. (6)

2 God told Abraham to sacrifice his son Isaac so Abraham set out with Isaac and his servants. When they came to the region of Moriah he told his servants to wait while he and Isaac went up the mountain. Isaac said to his father, 'We have the wood and the fire but where is the lamb for the burnt offering?' Abraham told him that God would provide the lamb. At the top of the mountain Abraham bound Isaac and was about to kill him when an angel told him to stop. (6)

3 The angel called Abraham and he said, 'Here I am.' Then he told Abraham not to kill Isaac because he had seen how much Abraham feared God and how Abraham would not keep his only son from God. Then the angel said that because of Abraham's faith God would bless him with as many descendants as stars in the sky and sand on the seashore. They would conquer their enemies and through him all nations would be blessed. (6)

4 Abraham took Isaac and his servants to the region of Moriah, where he left the servants and went up the mountain with Isaac. He was about to kill his son when the Angel of the Lord told him to stop. Abraham saw a ram caught in a thicket and he sacrificed that instead. The angel told Abraham that he would be blessed with numerous descendants who would become a great nation and be a blessing to all people. (6)

5 As they were going up the mountain, Isaac said, 'Father,' and Abraham replied, 'Yes my Son.' Isaac commented on the fact that they had the wood and the fire but wondered where the lamb for the burnt offering was. Abraham told him that the Lord would provide the lamb for the sacrifice. Then they went on together. (6)

Part c questions:

1 The story teaches that having faith means keeping God's covenant and being obedient to Him. Abraham obeyed God when He asked him to sacrifice his son. It teaches that faith means trusting God. Abraham trusted that God would somehow still fulfil His promise that he would be the father of a great nation, even if Isaac were to die. Lastly the story teaches that faith brings rewards. God rewarded Abraham with the promise of many descendants and land. (6)

2 The story teaches that Abraham was a man of great faith. He was prepared to sacrifice his only son and trust that God would still fulfil his promise that he would become the father of

a great nation. It teaches that he is obedient. God told him to sacrifice Isaac and he would have done so had the angel not stopped him. It also teaches us that he was a man of his time. Child sacrifice was common and Abraham did not see God's command as unusual. (6)

3   The covenant is the agreement between God and his people. God promises to love and protect his people if they obey him and keep His Commandments. In this story, God tests Abraham to see if he will obey Him by doing something that is extremely difficult. Abraham's faith in God proves that he trusts in God's covenant. In return, God promises that Abraham will have many descendants. (6)

4   This story teaches that God can be trusted to keep his covenant. He promised Abraham that he would be the father of a great nation and He prevented him from killing his son. It also teaches that God rewards faith. He promised that Abraham's descendants would conquer their enemies. It teaches that He wants obedience rather than sacrifice. Lastly it teaches that God has long-term plans. He said that through Abraham all nations would be blessed. (6)

5   The story teaches that making sacrifices is hard. Abraham loved his son and being prepared to offer him up to God in this way would have been very difficult. It also teaches that sacrifice can bring great rewards. Abraham's obedience was rewarded by promises for the future. Finally it teaches that sacrifice is not as important as the motive behind it. Abraham's actions were motivated by faith in God and desire to please and obey Him. (6)

Part d questions:

1   Some people think that the only important part of being a Christian is to believe in God and try to lead a good life. They think that making sacrifices, such as giving money to charity when it means doing without something themselves, is only optional. They will still go to heaven.

On the other hand, many Christians see sacrificial living as a key part of their life of service to God. Jesus taught that following him meant being prepared to give things up, even life itself. There are many Christians today who live like this, such as Jackie Pullinger in Hong Kong, Meg Guillebaud in Rwanda and people who work for organisations such as the Salvation Army.

I think that giving things up should not be optional for Christians as Jesus himself commanded them to take up their cross and follow him. (7)

2   If you don't look at this only in terms of money, the statement is true because the more you give, the happier you often are. If you are generous it encourages others to be generous towards you and towards others. Helping organisations like A Rocha, for example, makes you feel fulfilled because what you are doing is worthwhile.

On the other hand, the statement is obviously false because whatever you give to others, whether in time or money, you don't get back. Money you donate to charity is money you can't use for a holiday. Some people give up their time to work in deprived areas, for example, and at the end they are exhausted and depressed.

However, I agree with the statement. You only have to look at the joy in Jackie Pullinger's life to know that even though she was often discouraged and had her efforts thrown back at her, she received great blessings. (7)

3   Some people would argue that if God has commanded something, it cannot be wrong. Therefore by being prepared to kill his son, Abraham was not doing anything wrong but rather being obedient to God. It is also worth noting that in the end God did not actually require Abraham to kill Isaac.

On the other hand, it is dangerous to act on what you believe God might be saying to you if it affects others. Muslim extremists, for example, believe God is pleased when they kill innocent people in the name of Islam. In this way, Abraham is no different and he should have questioned what he thought was God's voice.

In conclusion, Abraham's actions were not wrong. He did not kill an innocent person even though he had been prepared to do so. He was a man of his day and he learned that his God was different and did not require human sacrifice. (7)

4   On the one hand, if it is God who commands us to do something, we should always do it. God commands us to love our neighbours and to give generously. He says we should help the poor and people in prison. Sometimes people believe He tells them to do a particular thing such as go and work in another country. Trevor Huddleston believed God told him to go to South Africa and work with people suffering injustice under the Apartheid system.

On the other hand, it is not always easy to know if it is God commanding you or just your own thoughts. Religious extremists sometimes think God is asking them to do something to hurt others, for example the Muslim extremists who blew up the bus in London in July 2005. In those cases it would not be right to 'obey God'.

In conclusion, we should always do what God commands but if it would hurt others we should assume it is not God's voice. (7)

5   Abraham is famous for his righteousness and great faith. Therefore he is a good role model for us today. He obeyed God as we should do. He trusted God in the important things in his life and for his future. People who have great faith in God inspire others to do great things so this makes Abraham a good role model.

On the other hand, it is dangerous to model oneself on someone whose life and culture are so different from our own. To Abraham, the idea of sacrificing his son was not strange or wrong, but to us it is. Therefore we should not take him as our role model in today's world.

In conclusion, it is Abraham's faith in God, his courage and the fact that he was prepared to make great personal sacrifice that we should copy. Therefore I agree with the statement, but within the context of the modern world. (7)

1.5 The Exodus and Passover

Part a questions:

1   Moses was the man chosen by God to lead the Israelites out of Egypt and was given the law (or Torah) by God at Sinai. (2)

2   A covenant is an agreement between God and His people. (2)

3   Salvation is being saved and being brought into a relationship with God. (2)

4   Exodus means going out and refers to the Israelites leaving Egypt. (2)

5   Sacrifice is giving something up for something of greater value. (2)

Part b questions:

1   Every Israelite family took an unblemished lamb (or goat) and killed it in the evening of the Passover. They painted its blood on the door posts of their houses as a sign to God that it was an Israelite house. After roasting the lamb they ate it quickly with bitter herbs. That night God passed over all the households in Egypt and killed all the first-born of the land – except those with the blood painted on the door posts. (6)

2   The Israelites had to kill a perfect yearling lamb, or goat, at twilight on the fourteenth day. They had to smear its blood on the doorposts and lintels of their houses. That night they had to roast the lamb whole over a fire, and eat it with bitter herbs and unleavened bread. None of the meat was to be left over. They had to eat with their cloaks tucked into their belts and sandals on their feet and a staff in their hand.   (6)

3   The Passover meal consisted of a whole roasted lamb, bitter herbs and unleavened bread. The meat was not to be eaten raw, nor was it to be cooked in water and nothing was to be left over. Anything that was not eaten was to be burnt. The people were to eat ready for travel with their cloaks tucked into their belts, their sandals on and a staff in their hand.   (6)

4   The Israelites ate the special meal on the night of the first Passover. The Lord passed over the land of Egypt killing every male, both human and animal. He also brought down judgement on the Egyptian gods. He saw the sign of the blood on the doors of the Hebrew houses and passed over them, allowing no evil plague to touch them.   (6)

Part c questions:

1   The covenant is God's agreement with His people. God promises to be faithful to His people if they obey His Commandments. In the Exodus, God is faithful because He acts through miracles, such as the passing through the Red Sea. The Exodus also teaches that the covenant is about freedom and hope because the Israelites were slaves and when they travelled to the Promised Land they were free. Finally, the Exodus reminds the people of their covenant duties when God gives Moses the Ten Commandments at Sinai.   (6)

2   The lamb was specially chosen and had to be without blemish. Roasting it whole and burning the leftovers showed that the Israelites were committed to escaping. The bitter herbs symbolised both their misery as slaves and their new freedom. The bread was unleavened because there was no time to bake properly and it would keep longer in the desert without yeast.   (6)

3   The Passover lamb was important because it symbolised the commitment of the Israelites to escaping. By killing the best of their young flocks they were putting their trust in God. The blood of the lamb was a symbol of God's saving power. For Christians, Jesus is often referred to as the Passover lamb because his death and blood saved people from slavery to sin.   (6)

4   The bitter herbs symbolised the misery the Israelites experienced as slaves. Eating them on that night represented freedom from that slavery and the chance of a new life. The unleavened bread symbolised the haste with which the preparations had to be made. There was no time to wait for yeast to work. The bread would also keep for many more days than leavened bread.   (6)

5   The saving nature of God is seen in the events of the Passover. The Israelites were spared death because of the blood on their doors. God kept His covenant with His people and freed them from slavery. God is also seen as a God of judgement because He punished the Egyptians for not letting the Israelites go.   (6)

Part d questions:

1   If God is all powerful and all loving then it would be wrong for Him to take sides. From His perspective, all people do good and bad things so it would be very odd for Him to favour some and not others. God must treat all people equally according to what they deserve.

However, if taking sides means being on the side of justice and truth then God has no option but to be biased. God could hardly take sides with someone who deliberately commits evil because that would suggest that He approves of evil – and that would mean He wasn't all good.

Therefore I think that God should take sides when it means making the world a fairer place. (7)

2   Sometimes the weak make their own problems. They do not help themselves improve their lot in life. They are content to let others do the work and then are surprised when they are left behind. God gives people opportunities and expects them to make the most of them. In this sense, it would not be true to say He sides with the weak.

On the other hand, others would agree that God always sides with the weak because they are usually the ones who are oppressed. The story of Moses shows how God sided with the Israelites against the mighty Egyptians. Throughout history He has used people to champion the weak. William Wilberforce, for example, campaigned for an end to the slave trade. The message of Jesus is one of hope for the weak, the poor and the oppressed.

In conclusion, therefore, I agree with the statement. God is on the side of weak where they are victims of exploitation and injustice. (7)

3   The Bible shows God as one who upholds justice. He heard Abel's blood crying out from the ground. He heard the cries of the Israelite slaves, and he sent Moses to rescue them. If God fights for justice then it is always worth fighting for. Oscar Romero came to believe this when he realised that the victims of injustice cannot help themselves.

On the other hand, it is sometimes better to leave things alone if there is no chance of winning. You might even make the situation worse. One of the criteria for a just war is whether there is a reasonable chance of victory. Tackling a bully by yourself may not be sensible.

My conclusion is that while justice is something we should try to uphold, we have to be careful how we go about fighting for it. Sometimes it is better to wait until we have more support. Therefore I cannot agree fully with the statement. (7)

4   Jews all over the world would agree with this statement. The Passover reminds them that God keeps His covenant, that He is still their God and as powerful today as He was at the time of Moses. Even though he is not a Jew, Barack Obama recognises the significance of the Passover ritual and by celebrating it he also remembers the abolition of slavery in America. The Passover symbolises freedom for the oppressed.

On the other hand, it all happened a long time ago and if you are not Jewish it has little relevance or significance. Rituals lose a lot of their importance over the years, rather like Christmas, and become merely a time for having fun.

My conclusion, however, is that the Passover has real significance today and it is a time when every Jew can think about their faith and their roots as a nation. (7)

5   One of the things that celebrating the Passover does is bring people together. It reminds the Jews especially of their national and spiritual identity. It brings the focus of the community back to God and reminds them of His power and that they are His people. It has helped them through very difficult times, such as the holocaust of the last century. They know that God is with them just as He was 3000 years ago.

On the other hand, simply remembering an event from so long ago is rather meaningless in today's world. Israel is an established country and Jews can also live safely in other places. They should get on with living in the present and not spend time reliving their ancient past.

On balance, although the Passover happened so long ago, it still serves a useful purpose today. It reminds everyone, not just the Jews, that God is still with them and will intervene to save them. (7)

1.6 The Ten Commandments

Part a questions:

1 A covenant is an agreement between God and His people. (2)

2 Worship is giving God praise and honour. (2)

3 Sinai is the holy Mountain of God. (2)

4 Justice is treating others fairly. (2)

5 Sabbath is the Jewish day of rest. (2)

Part b questions:

1 One religious Commandment is not to make any graven images of anything in the world and not to bow down to idols nor worship them. Another religious Commandment is not to take the name of God in vain. Two social Commandments are to honour one's parents and not to desire anything that belongs to someone else. (6)

2 Moses went up the mountain and God spoke to him. He told Moses to remind the Israelites how He had rescued them from Egypt and ask them if they would obey Him. If they did they would be God's treasured possession. They would be a kingdom of priests and a holy nation. Moses asked the people and they said they would. So God gave Moses the Ten Commandments. (6)

3 The first Commandment is to have no other gods before the God of Israel. The second is not to bow down to or worship any god but the God of Israel. The third Commandment is not to misuse the name of God. The fourth is to remember the Sabbath Day and keep it holy by not doing any work. (6)

4 The Commandments dealing with social behaviour are that people should honour their parents so their lives will be long. They should not murder or commit adultery. They should not steal and they should not give false testimony against their neighbour. Lastly they should not covet what is not theirs. (6)

5 The first four Commandments deal with religious observance. The Israelites were not to have any gods in addition to their own God. They were not to bow down or worship any gods except God and they were not to make idols in the form of anything on the earth or in heaven. They were not to misuse God's name and they were to keep the Sabbath Day holy, doing no work at all. (6)

Part c questions:

1 Firstly, the Commandments tell us that He is a jealous God. There must be no other gods but Him. Secondly, He is spirit because He cannot be represented by an idol. Thirdly, He is powerful because it is dangerous to use His name in vain. The Commandments about social behaviour show He is a loving God who wants His people to live in harmony. They show God is just and people should therefore strive for truth and honour. (6)

2   A covenant is an agreement between two parties; in this case between God and His people. God promised to protect them and lead them and He would make them His treasured possession above all nations. The Israelites, for their part, would obey God's laws, which were laid down in the Ten Commandments. If either God or the people failed to keep their side of the agreement then the covenant would be broken. That is why the Ten Commandments are a covenant. (6)

3   The first Commandment is important because it holds all the other Commandments together. All around the Israelites were other cultures with their own gods. Israel would soon lose her identity if she worshipped other gods. The Commandment not to covet is another important law because it deals with motives. Envy can lead to theft, murder and adultery so by keeping this law one would be keeping several others. (6)

4   The last Commandment deals with people's motives. Coveting is envy of something that belongs to another person and if not checked can lead to breaking more laws. Envy can lead to murder, theft and adultery and it can make someone lie in a court of law. Another reason this Commandment is important is that it shows that God looks at the heart and not just at outward behaviour. (6)

5   The Ten Commandments are given to Israel because they are a holy nation and to keep them as a holy nation. The word 'holy' means 'separate' or 'apart' and God chose Israel to be different from all other nations. God gave them the Ten Commandments so that they would live as a nation united by belief in God and holy because they were to behave differently.   (6)

Part d questions:

1   Some people might say that if you only had two Commandments you might not learn how to love your neighbour. You might decide yourself what loving them meant and break one of the Ten Commandments when you thought you were acting out of love. For example, you might think it was all right to commit adultery because you loved the other person.

Others say that if you love God, you will not offend Him by worshipping other gods or misusing His name. If you love your neighbour you will respect them and not want to harm them in any of the ways outlined by the Commandments. Just before Jesus told the parable of the Good Samaritan, the lawyer summed up the Law as loving God and your neighbour.

Therefore, I agree with the statement because loving God covers religious life, and loving your neighbour covers social living. (7)

2   In many ways this is true because as soon as we are told not to do something it becomes what we most want to do. For example, signs telling us not to walk on the grass make us want to tread on the grass. Rules often put ideas into our heads that we would not have had were it not for the rule forbidding it. We also don't like being told what to do and we use our independence by deliberately disobeying.

However, this is to misunderstand the purpose of rules. Rules help us to understand what sin is. If there were no rules, how would we know how to behave? Having rules sets a standard for morality today just as it did for the ancient Israelites.

Therefore, although having rules does encourage some people to break them, they are a necessary part of living in a civilised community. So I disagree with the statement. (7)

3   On the surface this looks like a valid statement because God is more important than anyone else. Loving God is the first Commandment, therefore the most important in God's eyes. Everything else stems from our love for God. We try to live good lives because we love God.

On the other hand, loving God means obeying Him and He tells us to love others. So if we do not love our neighbour we cannot love God properly. The Old Testament sums up the Law as 'Love God and love your neighbour.' The two cannot be separated. In the Parable of the Good Samaritan, Jesus commended the actions of the Samaritan who showed love for his neighbour, in sharp contrast to the lack of action of the priest and Levite who may have been going to the Temple to worship God.

Therefore I disagree with the statement because you cannot do one without the other. (7)

4 Most people would argue that the right to life is the most fundamental right of all. Every culture from the beginning of time has laws in place to protect it. Murder is still considered the most serious crime and carries the death penalty in many countries. Legal issues concerning abortion deal directly with the question of whether it is an infringement of the right to life.

On the other hand, some people might say that it is only more important in the light of other things such as freedom and happiness. A pregnant woman's right to live a happy life might seem to be greater than the right of her unborn child to live. Many people also think that executing a murderer is justifiable, which would make the right to life of less importance than other people's right to live in safety.

On balance, however, I agree with the statement because the right to life is the basis for all other rights. (7)

5 Most people would say that rules can occasionally be broken, particularly in life and death situations. For example, the rule that forbids you to drive over 70 mph becomes irrelevant when taking a very ill person to hospital. If you are starving, stealing food might not be considered wrong. Even Jesus broke the rules when he healed people on the Sabbath.

On the other hand, rules are there for a reason and they should not depend on someone's opinion about their relevance in a particular situation. The law expects you to keep the rules in all circumstances because society would fall into chaos if everyone ignored the rules or only kept to the ones they liked.

However, to say that rules should never be broken makes rules more important than people and that is not the purpose of law. Therefore I disagree with the statement. (7)

Theme 2: Leaders and prophets of the Old Testament

1.7 Moses

Part a questions:

1 The burning bush was a bush Moses saw that was on fire but not burning. (2)

2 A miracle is an act of God that breaks the laws of physics. (2)

3 Exodus means going out and refers to the Israelites leaving Egypt. (2)

4 Horeb is the holy Mountain of God, sometimes called Sinai. (2)

5 Salvation is being saved and brought into a relationship with God. (2)

Part b questions:

1 God told Moses that He was concerned about the suffering of His people in Egypt. He told him to go to Pharaoh. Moses was reluctant and said people would ask who had sent him. God told him to say 'I AM has sent me.' Moses was also to say that every generation was to remember this name. God told him to gather the elders and tell them that God would lead them out of Egypt and take them to a land flowing with milk and honey. (6)

2 Moses was with his sheep in the desert when he saw a bush that was on fire but not burning up. He went to look at it and heard God calling his name. God told him that He had heard the cries of the Israelites in Egypt and He wanted Moses to go and ask Pharaoh to release them. He gave Moses the authority of His name. (6)

3 God called to Moses, telling him to take off his shoes because he was standing on holy ground. God said He had heard the cries of the Israelites and was sending Moses to lead them to a land flowing with milk and honey. Moses was afraid but God said He would be with him. God also gave him His authority. Moses was to tell the Israelites that 'I AM has sent me to you.' (6)

4 Moses asked about God's name and God said, 'I AM WHO I AM.' God explained that His name meant that He was the God of the Israelites just as He was the God of their ancestors Abraham, Isaac and Jacob. His name would give him authority over the Israelites and over Pharaoh. (6)

5 God promised Moses that He would rescue the Israelites from slavery in Egypt. He would bring them into a land that was flowing with milk and honey. God promised He would give them the land that belonged to other tribes such as the Hittites. He promised to be with Moses and that Moses would bring the people back to the mountain. (6)

Part c questions:

1 The story shows that God is holy because He asked Moses to take off his shoes in His presence. It shows His compassion for His people's suffering. It shows that God honours the covenant He made with His people. He introduced Himself as the God of their fathers. Finally, His name, 'I AM', shows that He is a living, active being as opposed to the idols of pagan worship, which were not alive. (6)

2 The significance of the burning bush for Moses was that God was present in the bush. Fire was a symbol of holiness and purity and Moses had to cover his face because he was afraid to look at God's glory. The burning bush was also significant because it marked a turning point in Moses' life. No longer would he look after Jethro's sheep but he would go and rescue Israel. (6)

3 God told Moses to tell the Israelites that 'I AM has sent me' for two reasons. Firstly, it was to give Moses the authority to give the Israelites instructions. Secondly, the name itself carried power because the God of the Israelites was a living, active being. The present tense means that He is the same powerful God now as He was to their ancestors and they can trust Him. (6)

4 In promising them a land flowing with milk and honey, God was giving them everything they needed. The milk would come from sheep and goats and the honey would come from the bees. This was traditionally how the hill country of Canaan was described and God was promising that they would return to it. They would not always wander but become a settled nation, overthrowing their enemies. (6)

5   Moses was unsure whether to carry out God's commands because he felt inadequate to go to Pharaoh and demand the release of the Israelites. Even when God said He would be with him, he didn't want to go back because he was afraid the Israelites would not follow him. He had been away for a long time and had left after killing an Egyptian.   (6)

Part d questions:

1   If Moses had not returned to Egypt and brought the Israelites out, they would not have wandered in the desert and come to Mount Sinai. God would not have given Moses the Law and they would not have established themselves in Israel. Their whole history would have been different. Therefore it is the most important moment, not just in the Old Testament, but arguably in the history of Judaism and Christianity.

On the other hand, one could pick any of the moments when God intervened in the lives of his people and say the same thing. Also, if God is all powerful He would have found another way of rescuing the Israelites if Moses had refused to go.

I conclude that it is difficult to single out any one event as being the most important and it would also limit the power of God to do so. Therefore I disagree with the statement.   (7)

2   It was Moses who travelled to Egypt and demanded the release of the Israelites of Pharaoh. It was Moses who organised all the preparations for the Passover and led them out of Egypt and slavery. God gave him the power and authority to do this but Moses was the hero of the Exodus. He did not feel adequate for the task but he did it anyway. That is real heroism.

On the other hand, without God telling him to go, Moses would have remained in Midian. It was God who heard the cries of His people and took action first. Moses was simply obeying orders and following instructions. Therefore some people might claim that all the credit for the Exodus should be God's.

I agree with the statement that Moses was the real hero of the Exodus because he had to take great personal risks to organise and lead the Israelites.   (7)

3   Christians and Jews share common spiritual roots. The prophets urged the Jews of the Old Testament to look after the poor and the oppressed. God helped the Jews to escape from Egypt when they were oppressed. They should now do the same for others in that situation. In the same way, Christians have the example and teaching of Jesus to do the same so they too should always help the oppressed.

On the other hand, it is difficult to imagine this is something that every Christian and every Jew should do in every situation where people are oppressed. This is a collective responsibility for which organisations like Amnesty International have been set up to work with the poor and ill-treated.

Therefore I disagree with the statement, although it is true that Christians and Jews have a special God-given duty to help the oppressed.   (7)

4   Some people would argue that we can know who God is because of what is in the Bible. Through His actions God revealed His nature. For example, we know that He is a compassionate and loving God because He rescued the Israelites. We also know He is faithful and can be trusted because He always kept the covenant. Finally, He revealed himself in the person of Jesus. So we can know who God is.

On the other hand, it is very difficult to understand even what is said about God in the Bible. People have different ideas about Him and interpret the Bible differently. No one has ever met God because He is spirit and every religion has a different view of Him.

Therefore I disagree with the statement. We cannot know who God actually is because He is not physical like us. Belief in God has to rely on faith rather than knowledge. (7)

5   There are many cases in the Old Testament where God revealed Himself in unexpected ways, such as the burning bush. God needed to catch Moses' attention. God revealed Himself to Elijah by speaking in a soft whisper rather than the wind, earthquake or fire as he expected. Each time it was because God had something special to say. When He revealed His power over death and sin, He raised Jesus from the dead. The disciples did not expect that.

On the other hand, I don't think He always reveals himself this way. Perhaps when something unexpected happens, people look for the hand of God in it and they don't notice Him in the ordinary things. God can reveal Himself in a simple act of kindness to a stranger or in the pages of a book.

Therefore I disagree that God always reveals Himself in the unexpected. I think we see His character in lots of everyday things that happen too. (7)

1.8 David and Bathsheba

Part a questions:

1   David was the King of Israel. (2)

2   The Ark of the Covenant was the sacred box containing the two tablets of the Ten Commandments. (2)

3   Sin is disobeying God and separating oneself from Him. (2)

4   Temptation is the desire to do something wrong. (2)

5   Uriah was a soldier and a Hittite. (2)

Part b questions:

1   David sent for Uriah on the excuse of asking him how Joab and the troops were and then suggesting he go home to his wife. However, Uriah slept at the palace gate. He told David that while the army and the Ark of the Covenant were at war, he would not go home. Next, David invited him to supper and got him drunk but still he did not go home. Finally, David arranged for him to be killed in battle by ordering Joab to withdraw support at the crucial time. (6)

2   After David saw Bathsheba on the roof he had an affair with her and she became pregnant. Because she was married, David tried to persuade her husband, Uriah, who was a soldier in his army, to go home so that the child would appear to be his. When he refused, David got him drunk and suggested again that he should go home. Finally, he had him killed in battle by withdrawing support at the crucial moment. (6)

3   David invited Bathsheba's husband Uriah to supper and suggested he go home. Uriah refused because he was a soldier on active duty and it would not be fair to his troops. The following night David got Uriah drunk and again tried to make him go home so that the baby might be passed off as his. Again Uriah refused. Finally David arranged for Uriah to be in the thick of the fighting without support and Uriah was killed. (6)

4   David sent a letter to his commander, Joab, and ordered him to place Uriah where the fighting would be fiercest. Once battle had been engaged, Joab was to withdraw all the other soldiers except for Uriah and his men so that they would be killed. So, Joab put Uriah in the front line where the defence was strongest. When the men of the city came out, Uriah was one of the soldiers killed. (6)

5   David had an affair with Bathsheba. She became pregnant and David tried to persuade her husband, who was a soldier in his army, to go home so that the baby could be presumed his. Uriah was an upright man and refused to do so while his men were fighting. Eventually, David had Uriah killed in battle.   (6)

Part c questions:

1   The job of a king at this time was to be like a shepherd to his people and to protect them from enemies. A king also had to uphold justice in his country. David did none of these things. He did not behave like a shepherd towards Uriah, but stole his wife and had him killed to cover up his sin. He was not at war in this story but resting on his palace roof while his people fought without him. He did not act justly.   (6)

2   The story tells us that David had a great weakness for women. It shows that, at this point, he had forgotten his responsibilities as a king as he should have been in battle with his men. It shows that he thought he could do what he wanted because he was king. It shows that he was dishonest in the way he tried to manipulate Uriah into going home and in the way he had him killed.   (6)

3   The story does not suggest that David felt guilty when he committed adultery with Bathsheba. Rather, it teaches that guilt can be overridden when a person's conscience is not working properly. Once he found out that Bathsheba was pregnant, David knew he had to cover his actions. This tells us that guilt often leads people to lie and hide their actions.   (6)

4   Uriah was honest in all he did in contrast to David's dishonesty. David tried to get Uriah to neglect his duties and go home to his wife so that he, David, would not be discovered as the baby's father. Uriah took his responsibilities seriously while his men were camping on the battlefield and he was on active service, while David as king should have been fighting.   (6)

5   This story teaches that monarchs should lead their men into battle and not stay at home while others fight. It teaches that God expects the same high standards of behaviour of kings as He does of everyone else. David's position did not entitle him to commit adultery. It teaches that kings have a duty of care towards their subjects and they should certainly not get rid of people just because they are inconvenient.   (6)

Part d questions:

1   On the one hand, the idea of a life for a life appeals to our sense of justice. If someone takes the life of another, it is right that he should lose his life even if he is an important person such as King David, or someone who killed for political reasons such as a member of the IRA. Execution is a unique deterrent and the only way to ensure that the murderer does not kill again.

    On the other hand, many Christians believe Jesus taught that people should show mercy. God had mercy on Cain, although Cain was a murderer, and gave him a second chance. On a practical level, execution is irreversible and the wrong person is sometimes found guilty. This happened to Timothy Evans in 1950 and he was hanged.

    I conclude that although murder is a dreadful crime, execution is not the right punishment. Two wrongs don't make a right.   (7)

2   On the one hand, there is still a strong sense of public outrage over crimes committed. People don't stand for injustice. There was a huge public outcry over the fraud committed by politicians in 2010. People certainly know the difference between right and wrong because they try to hide who they are when they are committing crimes.

Others might argue that you only have to read the newspapers and watch television to see that people have lost their sense of right and wrong. The riots of August 2011 showed people as young as ten rioting and looting. Children today are not given proper moral guidance, the Church has lost its influence and society has lost its way.

So, although people are outraged at the crimes of others, they do not look at their own behaviour. I think that they are beginning to lose their moral compass and, like David, forget why certain actions are wrong. (7)

3 Because of the media, leaders today cannot really have private lives. People expect a high standard of moral behaviour, especially from politicians. These are the people who are making important decisions about our lives and we have to know we can trust them. If they are dishonest in their private lives, they can be dishonest in the workplace.

On the other hand, no one would come out as being completely good if they were put under the media microscope and it is unfair to expect our leaders to be perfect. They need somewhere to be themselves, make mistakes and learn from them out of the public eye. Some years ago, the headmaster of a famous school had an affair with a prostitute that was made public. Does that make him a bad headmaster?

In conclusion, although people should have the right to privacy, today's media-hungry world won't allow it. Leaders must get used to being under the spotlight and make sure their private lives are clean. (7)

4 There is no reason why a bad person cannot make a good leader. In fact, sometimes you even need someone of dubious morals to lead in a difficult situation such as war. Most people, for example, would agree that Hitler was a bad man but he had vision, charisma and good organisational skills. This made him an excellent leader. If you can inspire people to follow you, even through fear, like Stalin did in Russia, you can run an efficient nation.

However, the statement implies that bad people naturally make good leaders, which most people would disagree with. You only have to look at Colonel Gaddafi's leadership in Libya to see that he was a bad man and that made him a bad leader. He took wealth away from his country and he oppressed his people. Mubarak in Egypt and Mugabe in Zimbabwe are two more examples of bad people who were/are not good leaders.

Therefore I disagree with the statement. Bad people can make good leaders sometimes, but in general to be a good leader you have to be a moral person. (7)

5 People today expect a great deal of their leaders and they would say what David did was very bad. He had an affair with the wife of a soldier on active service. Then he tried to cover it up and had the man killed in an underhand way. Society would strongly condemn him. People expect leaders to live moral lives. You only have to remember America's reaction to President Clinton's affair to see that is true.

On the other hand, others would argue that committing adultery is not a serious crime any more. They might say that committing adultery did not stop Clinton from being an effective leader and knowing how to rule the country.

Therefore, in the context of his day, what David did was very bad. He was in a position of power and he abused it. He also broke three of the Ten Commandments and, in doing so, broke the covenant. (7)

1.9 Nathan

Part a questions:

1. A prophet is a person chosen by God to speak God's message to the people. (2)

2. Justice is treating others fairly. (2)

3. A parable is a story or saying that compares the Kingdom of God with everyday human events. (2)

4. Nathan was a prophet and advisor to King David. (2)

5. David was King of Israel. (2)

Part b questions:

1. God sent Nathan to speak to David. Nathan told him a parable about a rich man who wanted the poor man's prized ewe because he had to entertain a traveller but he didn't want to use his own sheep. So he took the poor man's lamb and served it for dinner. David was very angry and said the rich man should die. Nathan said David was that man – he shouldn't have slept with Bathsheba. David confessed that he had sinned. (6)

2. There were once two men: a rich man who had many sheep and cattle, and a poor man who had only one ewe lamb. It was kept as a pet and fed at the man's table. It even slept in his arms. One day a traveller called on the rich man. The rich man wanted to have a feast for the traveller, but did not want to kill one of his own flock, so he took the poor man's lamb and ate that instead. (6)

3. The rich man kept a huge flock of sheep and a large herd of cattle. One day a traveller called on him. The rich man did not want to kill one of his own animals for the feast so he took the lamb that belonged to the poor man, even though it was his only animal and very precious to him. He had it prepared for his meal with his visitor. (6)

4. David said the rich man should die and also pay for the lamb four times over. Nathan told him that he was that man. He said that God had given him Saul's kingdom and He would have given him more if he needed it. He said that because of his sin, God would bring calamity on his family. David said he had sinned before the Lord. Nathan replied that God had forgiven him but that his baby would die. (6)

Part c questions:

1. Nathan was brave because he was only a prophet and the usual role of a prophet was to tell the king what he wanted to hear. In this case, Nathan told David what he did not want to hear, which was that he had committed adultery and caused a murder. Nathan was courageous because he took a risk by telling the parable. David might not have condemned the rich man, in which case Nathan would not have been able to condemn David. (6)

2. The parable showed David he had sinned because it was about a man who had everything stealing from a man who had practically nothing. The rich man represented David, who was wealthy and had many wives; he did not need to take Uriah's only wife. Just like the rich man in the parable who misused his power over the poor man, David abused the power he had over Uriah and even had him killed. (6)

3. The point Nathan was making was that David's behaviour was both selfish and broke the covenant. Like the rich man, David had everything. God had given him wives, his crown and his land. Like the rich man who should have protected the poor man in his town, David as

king should have protected Uriah. Instead, he broke the covenant in at least two ways and he abused his role as king. (6)

4   The parable teaches that one sin can lead to further sin. In the parable, the rich man was selfish in not wanting to take from his own flock and this led him to take the poor man's ewe lamb. It also teaches that sin has consequences. David burned with anger at the injustice of the sins in the parable and stated that the man should die as a result. The sins in the parable parallel David's sins with Bathsheba and Uriah, that one led to another and the fact that there are consequences as a result of these sins. (6)

5   Nathan's approach was unusual because, unlike many other Old Testament prophets, he did not confront the king directly. Instead, he told a parable that made David realise for himself that he had done wrong. He was also unusual because many prophets of his day would have told the king what he wanted to hear and not pointed out his faults. (6)

Part d questions:

1   If a criminal meets the person they have harmed then it might make it really clear to them how much damage they have caused. It might affect their conscience and then they would want to put right what they have done. Nathan's parable to David was a way of making him face up to his responsibilities. Some argue this form of punishment is good for repairing the damage done to society.

However, others argue that the point of punishment is to make the criminal suffer the same pain that they have caused. Meeting their victim is not punishment and probably would not work anyway. Many criminals just want to do their time in prison and get out.

I think that making a criminal meet their victim could work but only in a small number of cases. In most cases, the punishment has to be unpleasant enough to deter people from committing a crime. (7)

2   In a society where there are so many different ways of doing things, we have to be tolerant of other people. Trying to make everyone act and think in the same way can lead to racial and religious hatred. For example, trying to prevent Muslim women from covering their faces or saying Christians should not wear crosses at work has led to a lot of unrest.

On the other hand, the 'live and let live' principle has to have limits. People cannot just do what they like regardless of the effects on those around them. People have to behave within the law and, to a certain extent, within the culture of the country in which they live. An example is women covering their shoulders and legs in a Muslim country.

On balance, I agree that we should live and let live but only as far as our actions are lawful and do not hurt or deeply offend others. (7)

3   Nathan was not afraid to tell David that his actions were wrong. There are many people today, such as the Archbishops of Canterbury and York, who confront governments over issues they feel are morally or ethically wrong. Trevor Huddleston might not have seen himself as a prophet but he campaigned against apartheid in South Africa. His actions helped bring about equality for black people.

On the other hand, it is not the role of a particular group of people to be the moral conscience of the government. Anybody can have his or her say. The media publishes people's ideas about ethical issues such as assisted dying and abortion, so there aren't any 'prophets' as such any more.

Overall, I think there are prophets like Nathan today; it is just more difficult to identify them. You have to sift through what everyone says and decide who is acting in a prophetic role. (7)

4 One of the aims of punishment is reform and to help people understand that what they did was wrong. Punishment focuses the mind on a particular action and its consequence, making inner change possible. A child punished for stealing, for example, will quickly realise that stealing is wrong and may therefore stop doing it. This makes the child a better person. In the same way, former criminals can become responsible, law-abiding people.

On the other hand, punishment can harden people and make them more determined to commit crimes. They will just take more care not to get caught. If the punishment does not fit the crime, the connection between the act and the punishment is not made and the offender is no better off.

Therefore, early punishment of wrong-doing can make you a better person. Most children grow up to be responsible citizens because they learned right from wrong by being punished as children. (7)

5 Many people would say that most of David's punishment would be borne by others so it was not harsh enough on him. His wives would be dishonoured and his children would die by the sword. His new baby son would also die. God should have done more than threaten David's future. He should have demanded that David receive the death penalty.

On the other hand, the kingdom needed a king and David was still a good ruler even if his personal life was not good. God had made David aware that he had caused the suffering of others and what he needed to do was to repent and start again. David did this.

Therefore, I disagree with the statement. God was not weak; He was allowing David to make a new start, and the death penalty would not have achieved anything. (7)

1.10 Solomon

Part a questions:

1 Wisdom is the ability to distinguish between good and evil. (2)

2 Justice is treating others fairly. (2)

3 Worship is giving God praise and honour. (2)

4 Solomon was David's son and king of Israel. (2)

Part b questions:

1 Two prostitutes came to Solomon. One claimed that the child she was carrying was hers while the other said she had stolen the child from her after her own child had died. In order to find out who the true mother was, Solomon said that he would cut the baby in two and give a part to each woman. At this, the real mother cried out that this was wrong and the other woman could have the child. Solomon concluded that it was the woman who cried out who was the real mother. (6)

2 Solomon dreamed that God said he could ask for anything. Solomon replied that God had continued the kindness He had shown to David but that he was as a child when it came to ruling a kingdom. He asked for wisdom to govern his people and to distinguish between right and wrong. God was pleased and granted his request. He also gave him wealth and, if he obeyed Him, long life as well. (6)

3 Solomon offered a thousand burnt offerings on the altar at Gibeon. That night God appeared to him in a dream and said he could ask for anything. Solomon asked for wisdom to govern his people and discernment to know right from wrong. God was so pleased with Solomon's

answer that He gave him wisdom and also wealth. He said if he obeyed Him he would have a long life. (6)

4 Two women appeared before Solomon, each claiming to be the mother of the same baby; the other baby having died. He heard their arguments and called for a sword. He said that since they could not agree, they should have half of the child each. The false mother said that was fair but the true mother cried that the other woman could keep the child. Then Solomon knew she was the real mother and gave the baby to her. (6)

5 Solomon returned to Jerusalem after his dream at Gibeon. He made a sacrifice at the Ark of the Covenant. Then he was visited by two prostitutes, both claiming that each was the rightful mother of the baby they had brought to show him. Solomon said that he would cut the child in two and give one part to each of the two women. At this point, the true mother said that she would rather give the child to the other woman than kill her child. (6)

Part c questions:

1 The significance is that both women do not have husbands or a stable family life and would have been regarded as outcasts by society. They are used to surviving by having to live unpleasant lives; perhaps this includes lying and cheating. This means that Solomon knows that both women are just as capable of lying as the other. This makes it a very tricky situation. Having wisdom means Solomon takes a risk, hoping that the true mother does actually have genuine feelings for her child. (6)

2 We learn that Solomon was a religious man who loved God. He offered a thousand burnt offerings at Gibeon. We learn from his dream that he was a humble man who acknowledged that he was inexperienced in ruling a kingdom. He was ambitious because he wanted wisdom to do it properly. We also learn that he was a righteous man who wanted to be able to discern between right and wrong. (6)

3 Solomon's request in his dream shows that he knew what was required in order to be a good leader. He needed wisdom to rule and the ability to understand a situation properly. The story also teaches that a good leader needs a discerning heart so that he knows the right thing to do in order to bring about a just ending. The story of the two women shows that a good leader needs to be decisive and prepared to act. (6)

4 Solomon was wise in two main ways in his dealings with the two women. Firstly, he made sure he understood the situation properly by allowing them both to tell their version of events. Secondly, he read the characters of the two women accurately and took the risk that the real mother would never allow her own child to be killed. (6)

5 Solomon's dream was significant because it set the tone of his reign. It established his desire to rule in justice because he asked for wisdom to do that. As a result, he was able to judge fairly between the two women and his fame spread. It was also significant because it demonstrated that his heart was in tune with God and God blessed him with the wealth for which Solomon became famous. (6)

Part d questions:

1 Leaders need many qualities but what these should be really depends on the situation. For example, when Jackie Pullinger was working with the Hong Kong gangs what she needed as a leader was determination. She had to be brave and have faith in what she was doing. On the other hand, the Queen does not need to be brave but loyal.

However, true wisdom might be being able to know which quality is the most important one. A leader who has wisdom knows when to be brave, when to be loyal and when to take risks.

This is why Solomon asked for a 'discerning heart' so he could see what was the right thing to do at the right time.

I think wisdom is the most important quality a leader can have because it means not acting selfishly but for others; that is what people respect and that is why they will do what a leader asks them to do. (7)

2   Many people would argue that this was true because fame brings more rewards than wisdom. Everyone seems to want a share in today's celebrity culture. People will go on TV programmes like *Big Brother* and *Britain's Got Talent* in order to achieve celebrity status, and they copy the behaviour of celebrities.

On the other hand, the vast majority of people would hate to be in the public eye as celebrities are, even if part of it were fun. They are already wise. Most people would rather be wise when it comes to relationships, be able to understand big issues that face the world and make the right decisions in life.

In conclusion, therefore, I think that while much of the celebrity lifestyle seems desirable, most people would prefer to have the wisdom that helps them succeed in the lives they already have. Therefore I disagree with the statement. (7)

3   Wisdom is the ability to distinguish between good and evil and to make good choices in life. God himself commended Solomon on his choice of wisdom. Solomon's wisdom enabled him to make Israel a great nation and himself a wealthy man. It was not necessary to be good to achieve these things.

Being good means being kind and bringing happiness to others in what we do and say. It is also one of the characteristics of God's nature. You don't have to be wise to be good. Some might argue that it was not very wise of Jackie Pullinger to work in the Walled City among dangerous drug addicts but it brought about a tremendous amount of good.

I think that leaders need wisdom and it helps if they are good. However, most of us would prefer to be among good people even if they are not always wise. Being good brings you closer to God. Therefore I think that it is more important than having wisdom. (7)

4   Good leadership is knowing what is best for the people you lead and being able to bring it about. When you make a decision it needs to be based on that alone; personal benefit should not come into it. Decisions should not be about you and what makes you look good. Therefore many people would argue that a leader should put others first and himself second.

On the other hand, leaders who put themselves first often understand what others want because most people want the same thing. What is good for the leader is often good for everyone. A leader of a troop in battle wants to get back safely, so soldiers will follow someone who puts precautions in place to bring that about. Leaders in government want a stable economy so that they can prosper. The country wants that as well so, in this sense, a good leader does put himself first.

However, leadership is about service to others and this usually involves putting them before yourself, so I disagree with the statement. (7)

5   Solomon relied heavily on his understanding of the characters of the two women; if he had got this wrong he would have had to kill the baby. Many people would say it was lucky that one of the women was compassionate and prepared to give up her child and that Solomon took a huge risk. They might argue that saying you were going to divide the child was not wise because it put the child's life in danger.

On the other hand, wisdom is partly about being able to discern the truth in a situation, and Solomon's understanding of the nature of the real mother led to his using this particular method of arriving at the truth. It was not really taking a risk because he was a good judge of character.

Therefore, it was not just luck that led to a happy outcome, although that must have played a part. It was Solomon's God-given wisdom that influenced his actions and led to the truth. (7)

1.11 Elijah

Part a questions:

1 A prophet is a person chosen by God to speak God's message to the people. (2)

2 Baal was a Canaanite god. (2)

3 Horeb is the holy Mountain of God, sometimes called Sinai. (2)

4 A covenant is an agreement between God and His people. (2)

5 Jezebel was wife of King Ahab. (2)

Part b questions:

1 Elijah told the prophets of Baal to build an altar and lay the sacrifice on it but not to light it. He said he would do the same. The god who lit the fire would prove himself to be the true god. The prophets of Baal shouted to Baal to hear them, they danced and cut themselves with knives but nothing happened. Then Elijah made special preparations for his sacrifice and prayed to God to show His power that all Israel might know who was God. God answered by sending fire down and burning up the sacrifice. (6)

2 King Ahab had gathered all Israel and her prophets to come to Mount Carmel. When Elijah saw them all he said to the people, 'How long will you go on trying to worship two completely different religions? You have to choose either to worship God or Baal.' The people didn't answer. Then Elijah challenged the 400 prophets of Baal to a competition. Whoever managed to get their god to set fire to a bull sacrifice was the true prophet. (6)

3 Elijah left his servant at Beersheba and went into the desert. He sat down under a broom tree and begged to die. As he slept, an angel woke him and told him to get up and eat. Elijah found freshly baked bread and a jar of water. He ate and drank then went to back to sleep. The angel woke him again and told him to eat and drink so that he would be able to continue his journey to Horeb. (6)

4 God spoke to Elijah and said, 'What are you doing here, Elijah?' Elijah replied that despite all his hard work, the people had torn down God's altars and killed His prophets. Then God told him to stand outside the cave. A powerful wind came, then an earthquake followed by raging fire, but God was not in these. Then came a soft whisper and Elijah covered his face. Then he and God talked about the future. (6)

5 A powerful wind shook the mountain and shattered the rocks. Then came an earthquake and, after that, a fire but God was not in these events. Then Elijah heard a gentle whisper. He covered his face and God said, 'What are you doing here, Elijah?' Elijah said that Israel had abandoned God and killed His prophets, leaving only him. Then God told him what would happen to Israel and how Elisha would take over from him as prophet. (6)

Part c questions:

1 Elijah wanted to prove beyond doubt that Yahweh was God and not Baal. He rebuilt the old altar, symbolising a return to worshipping Yahweh. He used twelve stones to show that Yahweh was God of a united Israel with all the twelve tribes. He used so much precious water because he was confident that God was powerful enough to light the wet altar, and to send the much-needed rain. (6)

2 Baal had to be challenged because he was not Israel's god and if the people continued to worship him, they would lose their national and spiritual identity. Jezebel was leading Israel away from the true God and it would not be long before they were absorbed into the Canaanite tribes. They had to have a public demonstration of God's power and Baal's uselessness so that they would turn back to God. (6)

3 The story teaches that God speaks to people's hearts. God was not in the dramatic events but in a gentle whisper. It teaches that God is holy because Elijah covered his face when he heard God's voice. It teaches that God cared for Elijah and arranged for Elisha to take over his role as prophet. It also teaches that God will not tolerate worship of other gods. He sent Elijah to anoint Jehu and Hazael who would kill those who worshipped Baal. (6)

4 The story teaches that sacrifice is costly. A bull represented wealth. By pouring so much water over the altar Elijah showed how sacrifice involves trust. There had been a drought for three years so water was very precious. Elijah trusted God to send rain so he was willing to sacrifice the water. The story teaches that for a sacrifice to be accepted, the motives of the person offering it have to be right. Elijah wanted the people to turn back to God. (6)

5 Elijah learned that God speaks to the heart gently. He learned that God understood what he had been through and did not condemn him for running away. He arranged for Elisha to take over as prophet. He knew that God was holy because he had to cover his face in His presence. By being sent to anoint Jehu and Hazael, Elijah learned that God will act to protect His people from false gods. (6)

Part d questions:

1 Many people say that you only have to look around you to see the evidence of God's existence. The world itself must have had a designer rather than have come about by chance. Someone must have set everything in motion in the very beginning. It is logical to believe there is a God.

On the other hand, it is hard to believe that there is a God when there is so much suffering in the world. If there were a God, surely He would have done something to prevent diseases such as cancer, or stop disasters such as the earthquake in Nepal.

I think the strongest evidence for the existence of God is in people's lives. They claim that God changed them, and their lives of love and self-sacrifice are evidence of that. However, this is more about experience than logic so perhaps the existence of God is not about logic but about faith. (7)

2 Many would agree with this statement. The world is happy for people to believe whatever they like. They don't care as long as it does not affect them. Children no longer grow up with a faith of their own so do not feel threatened or worried about people who believe different things.

On the other hand, there is a very active anti-religious movement in Britain today. People such as Richard Dawkins seem to care very much what others believe and try to pour scorn on their faith. In some jobs you are not allowed to wear signs of your religion such as crosses because you must not offend those of other faiths. This suggests that actually people do care what others believe.

This is a difficult issue because at one level people don't seem to care what anyone believes; it is up to the individual. At a deeper level however, they don't like anything that challenges how they think, so I disagree with the statement. (7)

3 Jesus taught that you should love your enemies and do good to those who hurt you without resorting to violence in any situation. Martin Luther King believed that black Americans should have the same rights as white people. His campaign was conducted without resort to violence. Oscar Romero believed that working together was what changed people, not violence. He died for this belief.

On the other hand, many would say that there comes a point when only violence is effective. Nelson Mandela fought for racial equality and an end to apartheid in South Africa. His supporters would argue that it was only the threat and use of violence that brought it about.

My conclusion is that it is sometimes necessary to use violence to defend one's beliefs when these affect how people are treated – fighting for racial equality, for example. But we should be prepared to suffer for our personal faith without retaliating. (7)

4 The celebrity culture of today makes gods of people. We put them on pedestals and try to copy them. People worship what celebrities stand for and forget that under the glamour they are ordinary people. No one can ever live up to these expectations, for example the golfer Tiger Woods was found to have cheated on his wife. This makes these people false gods because they cannot bring lasting fulfilment and happiness.

On the other hand, celebrities offer a glimpse of a life that is not ordinary or boring. It makes people happy and gives them a purpose. Celebrities inspire by example. Angelina Jolie does a great deal for charity. Cheryl Fernandez-Versini shows by her life that people can rise above negative childhood experiences.

However, you cannot make gods of people because people make mistakes and reveal themselves to be just like us. Therefore celebrities are false gods. (7)

5 If you believe in God then it is true to say that everyone has experienced Him through their conscience. God gave the Law and it is our consciences that tell us whether something is right or wrong. When we think about doing something wrong, our conscience tells us and we feel uncomfortable. For example, Adam and Eve felt ashamed after they had eaten the fruit because they knew it was wrong.

On the other hand, if you don't believe in God what you experience through your conscience is the product of upbringing and social conditioning. For example, you know it is wrong to steal because community living depends on respecting other people's possessions. Your conscience is simply a reflection of social values around you.

I think that although we all have consciences, we do not all experience God in them because we do not all believe in God. (7)

1.12 Isaiah

Part a questions:

1 Sin is disobeying God and separating oneself from Him. (2)

2 Justice is treating others fairly. (2)

3   Sacrifice is giving up something for something of greater value.   (2)

4   Discrimination is acting negatively against someone or some people.   (2)

5   A parable is a story or saying that compares the Kingdom of God with everyday human
    events.   (2)

Part b questions:

1   Isaiah accused Judah of hypocrisy. While the people there offered sacrifices to God, they
    trampled on the rights of the poor. They were pretending to be holy but their actions showed
    otherwise. Their justice system was corrupt and they did not defend the fatherless or the
    widows, nor did they champion the cause of the oppressed. They lived violent lives and
    their hands were covered in the blood of the innocent.   (6)

2   Isaiah's message was that Judah's leaders were oppressing the poor and neglecting to care for
    the defenceless such as widows and orphans. People could not get justice in the law courts.
    Even worse than this, the leaders' lives were hypocritical because they offered sacrifices in
    the Temple but prayed regularly to God. They kept religious festivals but their hearts were
    dishonest.   (6)

3   Isaiah said Judah's leaders could turn back to God by seeking justice and learning to do what
    is right. They should encourage the oppressed and fight for the rights of widows and orphans.
    God said that if they did this even though their sins were like scarlet, they would become
    white as snow, but they needed to obey Him.   (6)

4   There was a vineyard that had been planted with great care. It was on fertile soil, it had a
    winepress and it was protected by a hedge and a watch tower. The owner expected good
    grapes but the vineyard produced only bad ones. So he decided to tear down the protective
    hedge and allow the vineyard to be destroyed.   (6)

Part c questions:

1   Isaiah's message is one of hope because God wants the people of Judah to turn back to Him
    so that He can forgive them. He says that even though their sins are very bad – 'like scarlet'
    – they shall be forgiven and made as 'white as snow'. He says that if they obey God and
    are willing to do what is right, they will live in plenty. The message is one of hope because
    everything can be put right; it is not too late to repent.   (6)

2   The main reason God criticised Israel's and Judah's worship was that it was so hypocritical.
    While they offered sacrifices, said their prayers and kept the religious festivals, they did not
    deal justly with the poor and they failed in their duties to widows and orphans. God looks at
    the heart and He said He hated their New Moon festivals and their burnt offerings because
    their lives were a lie.   (6)

3   Having blood on your hands means being guilty and Israel was guilty of oppressing the
    poor. The people's evil deeds and unjust behaviour made them unclean in God's eyes.
    Social justice was the main thing that was wrong with Israel. It did not matter how
    many religious rituals they carried out; until they changed their ways, they could not
    be righteous before God.   (6)

4   The vineyard represents Israel and Judah. The hedges and winepress symbolise God's care and
    protection for his people. The bad grapes represent the people who have broken the covenant,
    worshipped idols and lived self-indulgent lives at the expense of the poor. The tearing down of
    the vineyard symbolises the destruction of Israel. The thorns and brambles are alien ideas and
    customs that spread through the nation.   (6)

5   Isaiah saw sin as something that corrupts from within. It was turning away from God and breaking the covenant. It made a relationship with God impossible and God would not accept hypocritical worship. Their selfish greed led them to oppress the poor, and operate a corrupt system of justice. However, he also said that sin could be forgiven, however bad it was. 'Though your sins are as scarlet, they shall be white as snow.'   (6)

Part d questions:

1   Isaiah's message is as relevant today as it was then because there is still so much injustice even at the hands of outwardly religious people. Oscar Romero challenged his church in El Salvador on exactly the same grounds. The recent abuses scandal in the Catholic Church is another example of how priests can harm and still offer prayers. The message of God's readiness to forgive is also the message of the gospel. God will forgive all those who truly repent, just as he promised in Isaiah's day.

On the other hand, religious organisations today do a tremendous amount to help the poor and oppressed. It was religious pressure that put an end to slavery, for example. Martin Luther King is another example of a religious man who fought for the oppressed in America, and brought about racial equality.

However, despite much good done in God's name, I think that Isaiah's message is still relevant. Newspapers are full of examples of humans causing harm to each other.   (7)

2   The people of Israel were religious but they were not just and fair. God condemned them for it, so it would seem that the statement is true. Being religious is the behaviour that is seen on the outside, such as going to church. Isaiah and later Jesus both taught that treating others fairly and looking after the poor and the weak is essential if you want to please God.

On the other hand, if a person is religious in the true way that is from the heart, then being just and fair will automatically follow. Jesus said you should love God and love your neighbour as yourself. The more you love God, the more you love your fellow human beings. So being just and fair is as important as being religious.

My opinion however, is that being religious is often more about the outer trappings of religion and that is not as important as being just and fair to others, so I agree with the statement.   (7)

3   Old Testament prophets do not have a reputation for being encouraging. Elijah criticised Ahab for leading Israel into Baal worship, and Nathan condemned David for his behaviour, so Isaiah is not so different. False encouragement would not save Israel and it was Isaiah's duty to give the people God's message.

On the other hand, Isaiah's words about reconciliation between God and His people are very encouraging. Having condemned the behaviour of Israel and Judah, Isaiah shows them the way back to God. He promises that even though their sins were 'red as crimson, they shall be like wool.' What could be more encouraging than being told that even though you have made a mess of things, it can all be put right?

Therefore I disagree with the statement that Isaiah could have been more encouraging. The role of a prophet meant giving God's message to the people and Isaiah's words were necessarily truthful. Isaiah's message reminded them they had a loving and forgiving God, which should have encouraged them to repent.   (7)

4   In the old days sermons were often about hell and damnation. This focus on sin and the wrath of God gave religion, and Christianity in particular, a bad name. Some might say that Isaiah's message has the same ring to it. Israel was sinful and had turned away from God, and death and destruction would surely follow.

Another way of looking at Isaiah's message is to focus on the love of God. This counterbalances what has gone before and shows a way forward for Israel that does not lead to destruction. Isaiah talks of God reasoning with His people as in a court of law and offering salvation. A guilty people were being given a second chance if they repented.

Therefore I disagree with the statement. Far from giving religion a bad name, this shows it at its best by offering forgiveness and hope for the future. (7)

5 The role of a prophet was always difficult because he usually had a challenging message to give from God. Prophets had to be bold to take on such tasks. Nathan had to tell David that his adultery with Bathsheba was wrong. Elijah had to tell Ahab that he was leading Israel astray. Both men risked their lives to do this. Elijah even had a price on his head. Such was the importance of their messages, however, that it would have been foolish not to have delivered them.

On the other hand, some people would view this as foolishness. Who risks their life to give an unpopular message if they don't have to? Tradition says that years later, under another king, Isaiah was killed because his messages were so unpopular. His words in this passage are hardly friendly and as future events would show, had no effect on the people.

However, real courage often appears foolish in the world's eyes. It was not foolishness that prompted him to try to turn Israel from its destructive path, but boldness to tell the truth. (7)

2 Interpreting the New Testament

Theme 1: Jesus' teaching

2.1 Zacchaeus

Part a questions:

1 Salvation is being saved and brought into a relationship with God. (2)

2 Repentance is having a sincere change of heart. (2)

3 Zacchaeus was a tax collector. (2)

4 'Son of Man' is the term used to describe Jesus' role as the one who would suffer for others. (2)

Part b questions:

1 In Jericho, Jesus called Zacchaeus, the tax collector, down from a sycamore tree so that he might stay with him even though the crowd criticised him for going to the house of a sinner. As a result, Zacchaeus said he would give half his possessions to the poor and pay back four times the amount he had cheated anyone out of. Jesus said that salvation had come to Zacchaeus' house that day. He declared that Zacchaeus was also a son of Abraham and that the Son of Man had come to seek and to save the lost. (6)

2 Zacchaeus met Jesus when Jesus was passing through Jericho. Because there was a large crowd there and Zacchaeus wasn't very tall, he climbed up a sycamore tree. Jesus called to him and asked to stay with him immediately. Zacchaeus welcomed Jesus and, despite the criticisms from the crowd, he said he would change his ways and give back half his possessions to the poor and pay back four times the amount he had cheated anyone out of. Jesus replied that salvation had arrived at Zacchaeus' house that day. (6)

3 Zaccheaus was a chief tax collector working in Jericho. He was very well off. As he told Jesus later, he had acquired much of his wealth by cheating. One day he heard that Jesus was passing through Jericho and he wanted to find out more about this man. However, there was a large crowd and as he was short he had to climb a sycamore tree. When Jesus arrived under the tree he stopped and called out to Zaccheaus that he wanted to stay at his house immediately. (6)

4 Jesus was passing through Jericho. There was a large crowd there waiting to greet him but he stopped under a sycamore tree. Looking up, he saw Zacchaeus, who was the chief tax collector, and he said to him, 'Zaccheaus, I would like to stay in your house today'. The crowd was shocked that Jesus should want to associate with a sinner. But Zaccheaus promised to give half his wealth to the poor and Jesus said that as Son of Man he had come to save that which was lost. (6)

Part c questions:

1 The term 'Son of Man' refers to Jesus' role as one who would suffer for others. Jesus' actions brought him eventually to the cross. Jesus especially looked for sinners because they were the ones in need of salvation. He found Zacchaeus even though he was hiding in the tree. Jesus' purpose in the world was to save sinners and bring people into a right relationship with God. Jesus spent his time in Jericho with Zacchaeus who had repented, and not with the religious leaders. (6)

2 Jesus went to Zacchaeus' house because Zacchaeus was a tax collector who had repented. Tax collectors were known to cheat people of their money and they were considered to be religiously unclean. So Jesus wanted to show that the Kingdom of God does not discriminate and welcomes all, whatever they may have done. By going to Zacchaeus' house Jesus must have shocked everyone because as a religious teacher he was not supposed to associate with sinners. (6)

3 Zacchaeus is called a sinner because tax collectors were known to cheat people of their money and they were considered to be religiously unclean. Zacchaeus was probably very rich because he had a share in all the taxes coming into Jericho. The term 'sinner' referred to all those who were considered to be excluded from the Jewish Law. This would have included prostitutes and lepers. (6)

4 Religious people must have been shocked that Jesus ate a meal with Zacchaeus because Jesus was considered to be a religious person who respected the Jewish Law and Zacchaeus was a sinner. Eating a meal with a sinner would have broken many religious laws and would also have made Jesus religiously unclean. Zacchaeus was considered a sinner because as a tax collector he had grown rich on taking more than his fair share of taxes. (6)

5 Jesus calls himself the Son of Man because he wants to be seen as someone who represents all humanity to God. In the Old Testament the phrase 'Son of Man' referred to someone whom God could trust with His authority. Jesus might also have thought of himself as Isaiah's suffering servant who died in obedience to God's will and which caused the people to feel guilt and see the error of their ways. (6)

Part d questions:

1 As a result of Jesus' visit, Zacchaeus took active steps to change his life and to make amends for his sin. He had stolen from the people as a dishonest tax collector, so he promised to pay back four times as much as he had taken. In addition he said he would give half his belongings to the poor. This showed that he had an active trust in God for his future, which is what true faith is.

However, Zacchaeus may have been prompted more by wanting to be accepted by the community than by any faith in the promise of salvation. He may have depended on this one gesture of generosity and public repentance to achieve this rather than on any faith in God.

I conclude that the statement is right and Zacchaeus was showing true faith. Jesus himself recognised his faith when he said salvation had come to his house. (7)

2 Racial discrimination is wrong because it considers some people to be inferior merely because they have skin of a different colour or come from a country other than one's own. Discrimination can often lead to violence and be the basis of great acts of social injustice. Racial discrimination means that in society a person may not get a job or is not allowed to own property because of their race.

On the other hand, it is only when people are tortured or murdered that an evil really has been committed. This has happened because of race or ethnicity in places like South Africa and Rwanda, and people such as Trevor Huddleston spent many years trying to stop it. Evil is always committed when people are treated as less than human.

I think racism is not the greatest evil in itself. The greatest evil is committed when humans are destroyed because they are not regarded as humans. Racism may be one cause for this but it is not the only reason.

(7)

3 Zacchaeus did deserve to be forgiven because he clearly showed remorse for what he had done and repented. Jesus taught in the Lord's Prayer that we should forgive others as God forgives us and so when Zacchaes said that he would give half his possessions to the poor and pay back four times the amount he had stolen, these are signs that he really meant to change his way of life. The fact that Jesus was prepared to eat with him and be criticised by the local religious authorities confirms that he deserved to be forgiven.

But there are good reasons why Zacchaeus shouldn't have been forgiven so easily. Perhaps he wanted to be socially accepted and therefore he made these public promises of repentance in front of Jesus so the people would think he was being genuine. He hadn't at this point actually given away his money.

I think Zacchaeus did deserve to be forgiven. Saying sorry in public is not easy and it is better to be generous with forgiveness than to be too mean.

(7)

4 Martin Luther King is an example of someone whose words changed the minds of millions. He gave famous speeches such as the *I Have a Dream* speech that are still read today and remind people of the terrible injustice of racism. Words remind us exactly what it is that needs to be done. Jesus' parables are memorable even for non-Christians.

On the other hand, if Martin Luther King had not led the bus boycotts or if Jackie Pullinger had not worked with the youth in Hong Kong, society would not have changed. Jesus said 'by their fruits you shall know them'. He meant that we should judge people by what they do, not what they say.

In conclusion, although words need actions to back them up they can have a much longer lasting effect.

(7)

5 There is no law that says we have to help outcasts today but there are laws that stop one discriminating against them. A law cannot command a person to be moral but it can protect someone who is considered part of a minority group from suffering physical and mental harm. For example, disabled people are often shunned by society but the law protects them and ensures they are treated fairly.

But some would argue that we should follow the law of conscience. Conscience tells us that it is morally wrong to treat any person badly, especially those who are on the fringe of society. Jesus spent a lot of his life siding with outcasts because if all humans are made in the image of God then everyone deserves to be treated with dignity.

I think we do have a duty to help outcasts today and that duty is based on the law of conscience.

(7)

2.2 The paralysed man

Part a questions:

1 Sin is disobeying God and separating oneself from Him. (2)

2 A miracle is an act of God that breaks the laws of physics. (2)

3 Blasphemy is speaking against God or making oneself equal to God. (2)

4 Faith is having an active trust in someone or in God. (2)

5 'Son of Man' is the term used to describe Jesus' role as the one who would suffer for others. (2)

Part b questions:

1 When the man reached the floor of the house Jesus said to him 'Son, your sins are forgiven'. The lawyers present said this was blasphemy and only God could forgive sins. So Jesus asked them whether it was easier to tell the man to take up his mat and walk or to say that his sins were forgiven. As the Son of Man, he said he had authority to forgive sins and he told the man to take up his mat – which the man did. (6)

2 When Jesus said to the paralysed man that his sins were forgiven, the lawyers present were shocked. They thought that only God could forgive sins and that Jesus was committing the sin of blasphemy. However, Jesus knew what they were thinking and he challenged them. He asked them whether it was easier to say to the man 'take up your mat and walk' or 'your sins are forgiven'. As the Son of Man, he had authority to forgive sins. He told the man to get up and go home. (6)

3 When Jesus was in Capernaum the people heard he was there and a large crowd gathered round his house – so large that there was no room to move. Jesus was preaching to them when four men arrived with the paralysed man on a stretcher. As they couldn't get close to Jesus, they climbed up onto the roof and dug their way through it. Then they lowered the man on his mat. Jesus was impressed by their faith and said to the paralysed man that his sins were forgiven. (6)

4 When Jesus saw the paralysed man being lowered down on his mat by four men, he was amazed by their faith. He said to the paralysed man, 'Son, your sins are forgiven'. However, the lawyers standing nearby were angry and thought that these words were blasphemy as only God could forgive sins. Jesus could see what they were thinking and asked them whether it was easier to forgive sins or to heal. As the Son of Man, he had authority to forgive the man's sins. (6)

5 When Jesus saw the paralysed man he said to him, 'Son, your sins are forgiven'. This shocked the lawyers. They thought that Jesus was committing blasphemy as only God could forgive sins and Jesus was claiming to have God's authority. Jesus could feel what they were thinking and challenged them. He asked them, 'Which is easier: to say your sins are forgiven or get up, take up your mat and walk?' As the Son of Man, he had God's authority and commanded the man to get up. (6)

Part c questions:

1 Jesus spoke of himself as the Son of Man because he thought of himself as acting on behalf of all humans. Jesus based his life on Isaiah's suffering servant who was chosen by God to

teach humans about their sinful nature. As God's representative, or Son of Man, he suffered greatly and was eventually killed. So, when Jesus uses the phrase he is not being blasphemous when he forgives because he has God's authority to teach about sin and forgiveness. (6)

2   This story teaches two things. First, it teaches that miracles are possible for those who have faith in Jesus' authority and power to heal. Secondly, and more significantly, it teaches that Jesus' authority to forgive sins does not make him a blasphemer. Jesus shows that the lawyers are inconsistent and hypocritical. Even though they thought that illness was a sign of sin, they still allowed people to be healed but considered forgiving sin to be wrong. (6)

3   The lawyers were angry with Jesus because he said to the man that his sins were forgiven. The lawyers considered this to be blasphemy because only God could forgive sins and Jesus was therefore assuming the role of God. They were even angrier with Jesus because he pointed out their hypocrisy; they didn't object to curing a person, even though they considered that some illnesses were signs of sin. (6)

4   Jesus did not think he had committed blasphemy for two reasons. Firstly, he pointed out to the lawyers that if they didn't object to curing a person, even though they considered that some illnesses were signs of sin, then curing the man's illness and forgiving sins were equivalent. Secondly, as Son of Man, he had God's authority to represent Him on earth and that included forgiving sins. (6)

5   The lawyers thought Jesus had committed blasphemy because he had deliberately said that the paralysed man's sins were forgiven and only God could take away sins. The punishment for blasphemy, according to the Jewish Law, was the death penalty. They were angry because they believed that Jesus had committed a serious crime. (6)

Part d questions:

1   There is no evidence to prove that God can suspend the laws of nature to make something happen. When we say miracles occur in hospitals we just mean that science has helped doctors to do remarkable things that could not have happened a few years ago. This is not because God has suspended the laws of nature but because we understand them more.

On the other hand, if someone did recover from a life-threatening illness when doctors thought he would die, this could be because God has intervened and helped the body heal itself. This might be difficult to prove but there is no reason why it might not be true.

Although I think in theory miracles are possible, in practice what we call miracles are really doctors and scientists using their knowledge in amazing ways. (7)

2   Faith can be very powerful. It can motivate people to do great things for themselves and for others. Archbishop Romero was driven by his Christian faith to side with the poor in El Salvador and to offer them hope against a cruel regime. For other people, their faith can help them to cope with their suffering because they see it as having some purpose.

However, for many others, faith is an illusion. If a person is physically suffering then faith does not take the pain away. If anything, faith could make the suffering worse as it offers false hope. Examples of this can been when tele-evangelists say they can offer miracle cures for those who have faith in Jesus. In most cases, the so-called cures are very short lived.

I think it is dishonest to pretend that faith is a kind of medicine. All it does is offer false hope and cause great harm. (7)

3   Jesus said that there is no greater act of love than that a person should lay down his life for his friend. A true friend is one who is prepared to sacrifice his own happiness for his friend as

a sign of his loyalty and trust. This is why Judas' treatment of Jesus was so despicable because he was prepared to betray Jesus simply because he disagreed with Jesus' mission.

But should we help our friends if they have committed a terrible crime or are about to do something very bad? If friendship is based on trust then it has to be a two way relationship. It could be argued that someone who has lied or committed adultery is not worthy of one's friendship unless they are prepared to confess their faults.

I don't think we are obliged to help our friends whatever they have done. There are some bad actions such as cold-blooded murder or rape that would make it impossible to stand by someone. (7)

4   It is simply cruel and unfair to make someone who is terminally ill stay alive. If someone has a right to live, then they must also have a right to die. We allow people the freedom to make all kinds of decisions about their lives, so it is irrational to deny their right to die if they feel their life no longer has great value.

On the other hand, it can never be morally acceptable to kill an innocent human being, which is what voluntary euthanasia is about. If we allow euthanasia for terminally ill people, then we have broken the Commandment 'do not kill' and abandoned the basic principles of the sanctity of life.

I think it is wrong to help a terminally ill person to die. It is much better to help people die in dignity and offer them palliative care as Cicely Saunders did through her hospices. (7)

5   Jesus' answer to the lawyers was very clever. He knew that they would not object to him curing the man because it was not against the Law to do so. But he also knew that they would probably have thought that illness was a sign that he or his parents had sinned. Therefore his answer is showing that they are inconsistent if they object to him forgiving the man's sin.

However, Jesus must have known that his answer was provocative. He knew that only God could forgive sins and he was saying these words just to annoy the lawyers. Jesus probably knew that illness and sin are very different things, so he was just using the moment to make a point.

Jesus' answer was clever. By asking the lawyers 'which is easier...' he is forcing them to consider their religious views. I think that forgiving other people's sins or faults is much harder in some ways than offering a physical cure. (7)

2.3 The calming of the storm

Part a questions:

1   Faith is having an active trust in someone or in God. (2)

2   A disciple is a follower or student. (2)

3   A miracle is an act of God that breaks the laws of physics. (2)

4   Jesus told the sea to be quiet and calm. (2)

Part b questions:

1   After Jesus had gone to sleep, a great storm blew up and the waves threatened to overturn the boat. The disciples were afraid and woke Jesus up, asking if he cared whether they drowned. He immediately got up and rebuked the wind and commanded the waves to be

calm. The storm died down and it was completely calm. Jesus asked his disciples why they had been afraid and had no faith. They, however, were terrified and amazed at his power. (6)

2   At the end of the day the disciples were crossing the Sea of Galilee when suddenly a storm blew up. The waves were filling the boat. The disciples were very frightened and woke Jesus up. They asked whether he cared that they were about to drown. Jesus rebuked the wind and told the waves to be quiet. Then there was a great calm. Jesus asked why they lacked faith. They were amazed and wondered who Jesus was if the wind and waves obeyed him. (6)

3   It was late and Jesus had finished teaching the people. Jesus suggested that they should go across to the other side of the Sea of Galilee. They set off, but then suddenly a storm blew up. The waves were filling the boat but Jesus was asleep. The frightened disciples woke him up and asked him, 'Teacher, don't you care if we drown?' Jesus rebuked the wind and told the waves to be quiet. There was a great calm. Jesus asked them, 'Why are you so afraid? Don't you have faith?' (6)

Part c questions:

1   Storms are often symbols of the devil's power and of chaos. In New Testament times, demons were thought to live in the sea and the waves would have appeared to threaten both the lives of the disciples and their souls. Without Jesus, life is like the storm that tossed the boat. The great calm that followed demonstrates Jesus' absolute power over the natural and the spiritual world. The calm symbolises a life of faith in Jesus. (6)

2   The story teaches that Jesus has complete trust in God. As storms often symbolised the battle between good and evil, the fact that Jesus was asleep in the stern of the boat while the disciples panicked shows how he trusted that God would triumph over evil. The story teaches that Jesus also has God's authority. When Jesus rebuked the wind and waves they stopped immediately; this symbolises the power that God has over nature. (6)

3   Jesus told off the disciples because firstly they were being superstitious. They should have realised as fishermen that storms blow up quickly on the Sea of Galilee and die away. They should have known that there was no evil power trying to destroy them. Secondly, they lacked trust in God. If God is the creator of the universe then He is also in charge of the storm and would look after them. (6)

4   The disciples were unsure who Jesus was because one moment he was asleep in the boat and seemed to be unconcerned for them and the next moment he was commanding the wind and waves to be still. They hadn't realised that as God's son, he had been given His authority to command nature. In Genesis, God had created the deep waters so this story teaches that there is no separate power of evil; God is in control of everything. (6)

5   Jesus and his disciples react very differently. As soon as the storm blows up, even though the disciples are fishermen, they panic and imagine that the spirits of the deep waters are going to destroy them. They lack faith and accuse Jesus of not caring. Jesus, on the other hand, sleeps on the stern of the boat. He probably does not think there are evil spirits because he trusts in God the creator to bring them safely through the storm. (6)

Part d questions:

1   Miracles cannot be repeated so it is very difficult to examine them scientifically. Therefore, it is almost impossible to disprove them or make any scientific statement about them. For example, you cannot order a miraculous healing so that you can observe it. Science can say

how things usually behave and do not behave, so it can make general statements about miracles, but such statements neither prove nor disprove them.

On the other hand, many things have been called miracles but actually aren't. Modern medicine brings about 'miraculous' cures. The rescue of the Chilean Miners has been called a miracle but it was technology that rescued them and there was no miracle in the sense of an occurrence defying the laws of science.

I agree with the statement. Science, far from disproving miracles, is the main provider of them. Modern technology and medical research have cured illness, put people into space and freed people trapped underground. (7)

2 The chances of everyone surviving an aeroplane crash must be very low. Even if someone could explain all the conditions that allowed people to escape death this wouldn't stop it being a miracle. They would have to explain how all these conditions happened to occur just at that moment. It is quite reasonable to say that God had intervened to make them possible.

But many would argue that this explanation is not a miracle at all. For it to be a miracle, some law of nature or physics would have to be broken. Surviving an air crash may be very unlikely but it is still possible. For it to be a miracle it would have to be impossible.

I think it depends on what we mean by 'miracle' as to whether this statement is true or not. I think the first explanation is better than the second because if God really did break the laws of nature then the effects of a miracle would be far greater than is ever reported. (7)

3 Some argue that we need to believe in miracles if we are to have proof that God exists and acts in the world. Miracles need not be spectacular nor do they have to break the laws of physics; they just have to be signs that God is somehow part of human lives. That is why the miracle stories in the New Testament have such a lot of symbolism.

On the other hand, we need not believe that miracles actually happen. We can still believe in God because of the beauty and design of the world. Jesus can still be the Son of God because of his teaching and obedience to His will.

I think we do need to believe that miracles happen in order to understand that God can do things in the world and that He can answer prayers. (7)

4 For many Christians, Jesus' miracles do prove he was the Son of God because someone who could walk on water, feed 5000 people, cure blind people and raise people from the dead must have God's powers. Only God is powerful and knowledgeable enough to break His own laws of nature, so if Jesus can do the same, he must be God's son.

However, Jesus' miracles can be explained in other ways. He might have had the gift of healing but his cures might have been exaggerated. Perhaps his nature miracles were just coincidences and he used these moments to teach or make a point as he did when he told parables. Jesus was a teacher, not God.

I don't think miracles do prove Jesus was the Son of God. There is too much uncertainty as to whether the miracles happened as recorded for them to be used as proof. (7)

5 There is a difference between true faith and blind faith. Blind faith means doing anything even if reason and conscience tell you that what you are doing is probably wrong. For example, Peter Sutcliffe, the 'Yorkshire Ripper', believed God had called him to murder thirteen women and that he was just obeying His commands. True faith requires one to consider carefully what the implications are of one's actions.

On the other hand, others argue that true faith means you cannot use reason for everything. Faith in a friend, just as much as faith in God, means one has to make a leap of trust. Not everything can be rational, and true faith can often be difficult. This must have been the case when Abraham was asked to sacrifice Isaac.

I think that true faith needs to be different from blind faith. We must have reasons for what we do, otherwise we could think our actions are acts of faith when in fact they are prompted by our distorted imagination.   (7)

2.4 The rich young man

Part a questions:

1   A disciple is a follower or student.   (2)

2   *Any two of:* do not murder, do not commit adultery, do not steal, do not give false testimony, do not defraud, honour father and mother.   (2)

3   Salvation is being saved and brought into a relationship with God.   (2)

4   Justice is treating others fairly.   (2)

5   Sacrifice means giving up something for something of greater value.   (2)

Part b questions:

1   Jesus told his disciples that wealth made it difficult for them to enter the Kingdom of God. He said it was easier for a camel to pass through the eye of a needle than for a rich man to enter the Kingdom of God. However, Jesus also said that with God all things were possible. He said that anyone who followed him would receive eternal life and that in the Kingdom the first would be last and the last first.   (6)

2   Jesus replied to the man that he should keep the Ten Commandments. The man said he had kept these since he was a boy. Jesus admired him and told him that he had another challenge for him. If he wanted to inherit eternal life then he must sell everything he had and give it to the poor. He would then have treasures in heaven. The man was very upset because he had great wealth.   (6)

3   A man ran up to Jesus and, falling on his knees, asked him, 'Good teacher, what must I do to gain eternal life?' Jesus was surprised. 'No one is good, except God,' he replied. But he went on to outline some of the Ten Commandments and see whether the man knew them. The man said he had kept these since he was a child. Then Jesus challenged him, 'Go sell all that you have and give it to the poor.' The man's face fell, because had great wealth.   (6)

4   Jesus said to his disciples, 'How hard it is for the rich to enter in the Kingdom of God! It is easier for a camel to pass through the eye of a needle than a rich man to enter the Kingdom of God.' The disciples were confused and asked who then would be saved. Peter said they had left everything to follow him. Jesus reassured them that everyone who had made these sacrifices would be repaid many times over in the Kingdom of God.   (6)

5   Jesus told the rich young man that unless he gave his wealth to the poor he couldn't inherit eternal life. He then told the disciples that the rich would find it very hard to enter the Kingdom of God – just as a camel would find it impossible to pass through the eye of a needle. But those, such as Peter and the disciples, who had given up home, family and property, would be rewarded a hundred times over in the age to come.   (6)

Part c questions:

1 In the first century, people believed that wealth was a sign of God's favour. It was a reward for being righteous. By saying that wealth was a hindrance to getting into the Kingdom of God, Jesus was turning that idea on its head. People would also have been surprised at the choice Jesus gave the rich young man because they did not understand that giving to the poor was a vital part of righteousness. (6)

2 There are two reasons why the man thought he had lived a good life. Firstly, he had kept the Ten Commandments since he was a child. He therefore regarded himself as a religious person. He probably asked Jesus about inheriting eternal life because he wanted him to say publicly that he was a good man. Secondly, he knew he was good because he was rich. In those days, great riches were seen as a sign of God's blessing and a reward for living a good life. (6)

3 The story teaches that discipleship requires sacrifice. The young man was challenged to give up his wealth and Jesus told Peter and the disciples that they had to leave their families as well. The story teaches that although keeping to the Ten Commandments is good, the disciple will have to respond to other demands that God makes. Finally, the story teaches that being a good disciple means siding with the poor against injustice. (6)

4 This little parable illustrates the impossibility of someone who is attached to his wealth becoming a true disciple. It would have been a shocking parable because having riches was thought to be a sign of God's blessing and Jesus appears to be saying the opposite. The parable is very stern and is a warning to rich people that they will be unable to enter the Kingdom of God. (6)

5 Jesus meant that the Kingdom of God reverses what humans think is fair and just with what God wants. For example, among humans it is the rich and powerful who are regarded as the most important in society. But in the Kingdom of God it is those who are compassionate, generous and merciful who will be first. Jesus also meant that those whom society despises – outcasts and the poor – will not be rejected from the Kingdom. (6)

Part d questions:

1 Some Christians think that having money when there are so many starving people in the world is wrong. They say that because Jesus told the rich young man to give everything to the poor, it is right to give all their money away too. For example, a Cornish woman sold all she had in response to an appeal to help victims of a famine in Africa. She went to live in a caravan.

On the other hand, there are many Christians who say that if they do not have any money, they cannot help the poor and oppressed. Philanthropists, like Bob Edmiston, give away millions of pounds to charity, but keep enough to live on and sustain their giving. If we give everything away, we become a burden on society because we have to live on benefits.

I conclude therefore that Christians do not have a duty to give all their money away but they should use their wealth to support the poor. (7)

2 As Isaiah taught, a society that does not help the poor is corrupt. Using wealth wisely to help the poor and oppressed is a basic duty for religious and non-religious people. In Christian terms, Jesus sided with the poor because all people are our neighbours and require our help. In the parable of the Good Samaritan, Jesus criticised the priest and Levite for putting religion before people.

However, worship is necessary to give people a sense of God's presence. Religious buildings are there as signs of human praise of God and to remind us of His place in society. Worship of God is the basis of the Ten Commandments – there is no moral duty to help the poor first.

I think that spending money on places of worship is important. Some people argue that God can be worshipped anywhere but we need places that are special in order to do this. This doesn't mean that the poor are unimportant but worship of God should come first. (7)

3 Some argue that it is not the love of money that is the root of all evil, but human greed and selfishness. Some people are driven by their love of money to set up businesses and in competition with others to be very successful. If they did not love money they wouldn't seek to make better products or be more efficient. Society would not progress.

However, others argue that the love of money is not only selfish but also very dangerous. It makes things more important than people. It treats people as a means to an end, like a piece of machinery. It can lead to deceit and even murder. Tyrants love money and power and feel nothing about destroying others to get there.

I think the second view is over-exaggerated. This is what happens when love of money is the only love one has. It is possible to love making money and also to love people at the same time. (7)

4 All Christians should be poor because Jesus said very clearly that rich people cannot enter the Kingdom of God. He also told the rich young man to give away his possessions and he told the disciples to give up fishing and become fishers of people. Christians become monks and nuns, and give up their wealth to serve God and people. They wouldn't do this unless they thought it was their Christian duty.

But, on the other hand, Jesus wasn't telling all people to give up their wealth. He was challenging the young man to see if he really loved God or whether he really loved his riches more. Becoming a monk or nun is the exception, not the rule, in Christianity. What matters is becoming 'poor in spirit' as Jesus taught, meaning to be generous to others.

I think far too many Christians are unnecessarily rich and should use their money to help the poor. They need to be much more 'poor in spirit'. (7)

5 Humans are naturally competitive and if they don't have something to work for they lose their sense of purpose. Acquiring wealth, whether this is a home, possessions or a business, is just part of being human. Therefore, if Christian teaching suggests that we should give away wealth, it is not only unrealistic but wrong.

However, Jesus wasn't teaching that wealth is itself a bad thing. What he attacked was the attitude that all that matters is acquiring wealth. The early Christians took his teaching to mean that wealth should be distributed to all those who had need. Society need not be competitive to work properly.

I think Jesus' teaching on wealth is unrealistic. Humans need competition to feel worthwhile. We have seen how communism has failed and Jesus' teaching is very close to communism, so I agree with the statement. (7)

2.5 The woman and Simon the Pharisee

Part a questions:

1 A parable is a story or saying that compares the Kingdom of God with everyday human events. (2)

2 Sin is disobeying God and separating oneself from Him. (2)

3 The Pharisees were Jewish religious teachers who taught strict obedience to the Law. (2)

4 Faith is having an active trust in someone or in God. (2)

5 Salvation means being saved and brought into a relationship with God. (2)

Part b questions:

1 Simon the Pharisee invited Jesus to supper with him. While he was at the table, a sinful woman brought a jar of perfume to the house and stood behind Jesus. She wept so much her tears fell on Jesus' feet so she wiped them with her hair and poured perfume over them. Simon thought that if Jesus were really a prophet, he would know what sort of person the woman was. Jesus then told him the parable. (6)

2 When the woman heard that Jesus was at Simon the Pharisee's house, she arrived carrying an alabaster jar of perfume. She was crying and her tears wet Jesus' feet. She wiped his feet dry with her hair, kissed them and then anointed them with the perfume. Simon was shocked because Jesus didn't seem to realise that the woman was a sinner. (6)

3 A money-lender was owed money by two debtors. One debtor owed 500 denarii and the other 50 denarii. Neither had enough money to pay back what they owed. Jesus asked if the man were to forgive them and release them from their debts, who would love him more. Simon the Pharisee answered that the one whose debt was bigger would love him more. Jesus said that Simon had made the right judgement. (6)

4 While Jesus was having supper with Simon the Pharisee, a sinful woman arrived. She washed Jesus' feet with her tears, wiped them with her hair and anointed them with perfume. Simon was shocked as she was a sinner. Jesus told him a parable about two debtors to make the point that those who owe more should be forgiven more. Simon had failed in welcoming Jesus as a guest but she had shown great love. Jesus forgave the woman's sins. (6)

5 Jesus criticised Simon the Pharisee by telling him a parable about two debtors to show that we should show more forgiveness to those whose sin or debt is greater. Jesus then criticised Simon because, unlike the woman who had washed his feet with her tears and anointed him with perfume, he had shown Jesus little love when he invited him into his house. (6)

Part c questions:

1 Simon would have been embarrassed by Jesus' parable because he would have realised it was directed at him. By having to acknowledge that the one who loved more was the one who was forgiven more, he was admitting that his attitude towards the woman was wrong. He condemned her while Jesus accepted her and forgave her. The parable also made him see that his actions had not shown even the most basic courtesy, let alone love, towards Jesus, while this sinful woman had. (6)

2 Jesus showed compassion towards the woman even though she was regarded as a sinner (probably a prostitute). He knew that the Pharisees would not have regarded her actions as being religiously good because as a sinner she was unable to carry out the Jewish Law. But Jesus considered her actions to be more than enough to be a sign of her genuine repentance. His parable teaches that mercy and generosity are the basis of the Law. (6)

3 The woman is an outcast because she is probably a prostitute. That does not necessarily mean she is a bad person; there are many reasons that might have led her to this way of life. Jesus criticises Simon because he judges her based on his religious prejudices about sinners or outcasts. Jesus' teaching is that those who truly keep to God's Law are those who forgive most and show love towards others, not those who judge. (6)

4 The parable Jesus told is an allegory; the person with the greater debt represents the sinful woman and her great sin. The money lender who cancels debts is like Jesus who forgives sins. Naturally someone who has had a great debt cancelled will be enormously grateful and show

love in response. Simon, as a Pharisee, is so concerned with obedience to the Jewish Law that he does not comprehend the joy and love when sins are forgiven. (6)

5   The woman believed that despite her status as a sinner and a prostitute, Jesus would cut through the religious prejudices of his day and show her mercy and forgiveness. As a sign of her trust and devotion she was prepared to be ridiculed by the Pharisees and anoint Jesus with expensive perfume. She had made a huge sacrifice. Her tears showed her belief that her remorse and faith would be met by Jesus' love. (6)

Part d questions:

1   Asylum seekers are usually poor, often homeless and made to feel unwanted, and always at a disadvantage. Because they are exactly the sort of people Jesus came to seek and to save, it is the duty of every Christian to do what he can to help them too. Jesus never judged those who came to him and so we should not let prejudice get in the way of helping anyone in need, even asylum seekers.

On the other hand, some people say that asylum seekers are not always escaping persecution in their own countries, but are trying to make a better life for themselves in England. If we help them too much, large numbers of other asylum seekers will follow them and they will take our jobs and exhaust our NHS.

I think that we should always try to help people whoever they are, just as Jesus did. It is not for us to judge, although we have to be practical. (7)

2   The answer to this question depends on what we think the purpose of punishment is. If a small crime is one such as shop-lifting or small-scale fraud, then the person who commits the crime is not dangerous and society does not need protecting from them. Fines and community service might therefore be sufficient to reform such a person. This option is cheaper than prison and avoids the problem of prisons being 'universities of crime' where minor criminals come out knowing how to commit major crimes.

However, the problem with this view is that it does not deter others from committing crimes. If a person knows that committing even a small-scale fraud could place them in prison, then they might think twice about doing it. Furthermore, the criminal has to experience the harm they have done to others, and prison is a good way of making sure this happens.

I think that we have to acknowledge that people make mistakes and that prison is not always the best way of dealing with small crimes, so I agree with the statement. (7)

3   A hypocrite is someone who says one thing and does something else. I think, however, that we need to consider whether the person intended to have double standards before they can be called a hypocrite. In the case of Simon, he was a Pharisee and Pharisees tried very hard to carry out the Commandments of the Law so as to be as religiously good as possible. From their point of view, as the woman was a prostitute and had broken the law, perhaps Simon was right to think that she was a sinner and Jesus should not eat with her.

On the other hand, Simon would have known that his religious beliefs required him to show mercy, particularly to the weak and marginalised. He, however, had chosen to forget this.

I think it is impossible to be utterly morally consistent, but I don't think that makes everyone a hypocrite. Some people are hypocrites because they choose to have double standards, but most people are well intentioned but inconsistent. (7)

4   From the point of view of the Golden Rule, which says that we should treat others as we would have them treat us, then we would probably want people to forgive more and criticise less. This is because we all make mistakes and we don't need to be reminded of them; rather, we would prefer others to forgive us and allow us to put our mistakes right. A tolerant society is a much better place in which to live than a very judgemental one.

On the other hand, this view assumes that people realise their mistakes. If we didn't criticise, then people wouldn't change their ways. They might not think that what they were doing was wrong. Jesus criticised the Pharisees and Bonhoeffer bravely criticised Hitler and the Nazis.

It is probably true that it is much easier to criticise than to forgive. So, I agree that we should forgive more because that makes society a much fairer and happier place in which to live.   (7)

5   Simon was a bad person. As a Pharisee he believed that he was living a religiously superior life and had set himself high standards according to the Law. But by doing this he had put religion before his duty to show mercy and love to the weak. Had he read Amos and Isaiah properly he would have known this.

However, Simon was misled by his narrow religious views. He wasn't a bad person; it was just that he hadn't fully considered that the heart of Judaism teaches that justice extends beyond those who are religious to those who are marginalised by society.

It is difficult to know whether Simon was a good or bad person. If the story had told of Simon's reaction to Jesus' parable then we could make a decision. However, I think that he would have known what kind of person Jesus was and been prepared to change his ways. If so, that would have made him not a bad person but a misguided one.   (7)

2.6 The Good Samaritan

Part a questions:

1   A parable is a story or saying that compares the Kingdom of God with everyday human events.   (2)

2   The Samaritans were a group of people whom the Jews considered to be religiously and racially inferior.   (2)

3   Discrimination is acting negatively against someone or some people.   (2)

4   The lawyer asks Jesus, 'What must I do to inherit eternal life' and 'Who is my neighbour?'   (2)

5   'Go and do likewise' (i.e. show mercy).   (2)

Part b questions:

1   The man who had been beaten up by robbers lay on the Jericho road. When a priest came along he ignored the man and walked past on the other side of the road. Then a Levite came and he did the same. But when a Samaritan man saw the wounded man, he bandaged the man's wounds and took him to an inn, gave the inn-keeper money to feed and care for him and told him that if he spent more he would repay him.   (6)

2   A man was travelling from Jerusalem to Jericho when he was attacked by robbers and left to die. A priest was on the same road but when he saw him he crossed to the other side. A Levite did the same. But when a Samaritan saw him he took pity on him. He bandaged his wounds and took him to an inn. The next day he gave two denarii to the inn-keeper to look after the man and promised to give him more if he needed it when he returned.   (6)

3 Jesus replied with a parable. A man was travelling from Jerusalem to Jericho when he was beaten up by robbers and left half-dead. A priest came by but he passed on the other side of the road. A Levite did the same thing. Then a Samaritan came by and he saw the man and took pity on him. He bandaged his wounds and took him to an inn and gave the inn-keeper money to care for him. Jesus asked the lawyer who was a neighbour to the man. (6)

4 The man was badly beaten up by robbers, stripped of his clothes and left half-dead. When a priest was walking by, he crossed to the other side of the road. The same thing happened with a Levite. However, when a Samaritan traveller saw him, he took pity. He washed his wounds with oil and wine and bandaged them. Then he took him on his donkey to an inn and looked after him. He paid the inn-keeper to take care of him and promised to repay him for any extras. (6)

5 A lawyer asked Jesus what he must do to inherit eternal life. Jesus asked him what was written in the Law. The lawyer said that you should love God with all your heart, soul and strength and mind, and love your neighbour as yourself. Jesus replied that if he did this he would live. The lawyer wanted to justify having asked the question so he asked, 'Who is my neighbour?' This led to Jesus telling the parable.

Part c questions:

1 Firstly, many Jews would have said that 'neighbour' only referred to other Jews. So, as the Samaritans were not regarded as proper Jews but as foreigners, then the answer is a neighbour is anyone who does good things. Secondly, a neighbour is anyone whom we come across who needs our help. The priest and Levite ignored the wounded man because they used the excuse that they didn't want to touch a dead body and become religiously impure. (6)

2 Jesus often used parables because they could express in everyday terms complex ideas about the Kingdom of God. For example, in the Good Samaritan, Jesus wants people to understand what it means to show mercy, leave aside prejudices and to love one's neighbour. Parables are also easily memorable. A story or a brief saying can be remembered first and thought about later, such as the parable of the camel and the eye of the needle. (6)

3 The parable teaches that one's neighbour is anyone who has need. This means leaving aside prejudices and even religious duties and making sure that the basic commands to show mercy and compassion are followed first. In the parable the priest and Levite put their religion first because they thought if they touched a dead body they would become unclean. The twist in the parable is that the man whom the Jews despised as being racially inferior, the Samaritan, is closest to carrying out God's Law. (6)

4 Jesus chose a Samaritan because the Jews regarded them as being racially and religiously inferior. They thought that it would be impossible for a Samaritan to be able to carry out the Law because Samaritans were corrupt. But in the parable it is the priest and the Levite who are shown to be religiously inferior because they fail to show mercy to the wounded man. In the Old Testament God says that mercy is the foundation of the Law. So, Jesus uses the Samaritan to shock people into seeing this. (6)

5 The main prejudice the parable deals with is racial. Jews considered Samaritans to be racially and religiously inferior. They thought that it would be impossible for a Samaritan to be able to carry out the Law because Samaritans were corrupt. Yet it is the Samaritan who fulfils God's Law. The other prejudice is the way the priest and Levite discriminate against the wounded man because they don't want to become religiously impure by touching him. (6)

Part d questions:

1   Parables are not the best way to teach about the Kingdom of God because they can be confusing and their meaning unclear. For example, if you didn't know about Samaritans and their relationship to the Jews, then it would be difficult to understand that the Kingdom of God is about challenging prejudices. Also the parable might just be treated as a story rather than as something that has a deeper meaning.

     On the other hand, parables are memorable and they are there to make one think. Jesus often chose everyday events but presented them in unusual ways. For example, even if one didn't know about Samaritans, it is clear that religious people, who ought to know about the Kingdom of God, obviously fail to do good. This can make us think about the obvious things we fail to do.

     So, I conclude that parables are a very good way of teaching about the Kingdom of God because they are memorable and make us think more deeply.   (7)

2   All those who work to reconcile people probably feel that they don't actually like some of the people they are dealing with. The people may have done terrible things and have attitudes of which the people working to reconcile disapprove. However, they still think there is some good in them even if they don't like them. Meg Guillebaud must have felt this in Rwanda when she worked with the genocide victims and those who had done the killing.

     On the other hand, if one really doesn't like someone it is very hard to be genuinely kind to them. To do so would be to overlook their faults and perhaps very bad things they have done. It would be very hard to be kind to someone who had deliberately tortured another person for fun, for example.

     I agree with the statement. Perhaps if you are like Meg Guillebaud or Jackie Pullinger, both of whom had a strong Christian faith, you might get close to showing genuine kindness to those whom you do not like.   (7)

3   This is an odd statement. There are thousands of people who dedicate their lives to helping others. There are those who work with drug addicts, people in prison and down and outs. They often do so for nothing and give their time generously through charities. Some people dedicate their whole lives to being 'good Samaritans'.

     On the other hand are these people *really* good? People like Mother Teresa have many critics, who accuse them of being very selective about who they treat and of rather liking the media attention. Perhaps working for charities is just a way of making oneself feel better.

     In conclusion, I think there is nothing to support this statement. The critics of Mother Teresa and other 'good Samaritans' are setting a standard that is so high that no one, not even the Good Samaritan himself, could ever meet it.   (7)

4   It might be easier today to be a good Samaritan perhaps because, in the Western world at least, we are better off than in the past and have technology and other means to do good at a distance. For example, it is easy to give money to charities working in LEDCs or raise money for development agencies. Charities can advertise on the internet and news broadcasts can alert us to national disasters and those in need within minutes.

     However, so much information can lead to what some call 'charity fatigue'. People give up being good Samaritans because they are constantly being asked to give. Also, we get used to seeing disasters on television and we turn our attention to other things. Modern living often means we don't know our neighbours in the street so we are ignorant of who may need our help.

In conclusion, I think it might be harder for us to be a good Samaritan today as we have more and therefore are expected to be even more generous. (7)

5 There are complicated reasons for racism. People are racists out of fear of the unknown, anger because they think 'foreigners' are trying to take their jobs and suspicion because they worry their traditions and values are being destroyed. Jesus' parable touches on all these aspects. If racism is to end, people need to see those of a different race as fellow human beings.

But racism is by its very nature irrational. Even if someone understood all the background to the parable and could see how well the despised Samaritan had behaved, they might not connect this with their hatred and fear of others. Some might say that this is an example of *one* good Samaritan, but that the rest are still bad. Racism often generalises in this way.

In conclusion, I think the Parable of the Good Samaritan could change the attitudes of many people today, but it wouldn't wipe out racism in the world. (7)

2.7 The Lost Son

Part a questions:

1 A parable is a story or saying that compares the Kingdom of God with everyday human events. (2)

2 Repentance is a sincere change of heart. (2)

3 Salvation means being saved and brought into a relationship with God. (2)

4 Sin is disobeying God and separating oneself from Him. (2)

5 The younger son said, 'I have sinned against heaven and against you.' (2)

Part b questions:

1 When he came to his senses, the younger son thought how he would be better off as a hired hand on his father's farm. They had food to spare while he was starving to death. He decided to go back to his father and say that he had sinned against heaven and against him and was no longer worthy to be called his son. He would ask to be taken on as a hired servant. (6)

2 After the younger son had spent all his money there was then a severe famine in the land. He was desperate for work so he found employment looking after pigs. He was so hungry that he could even have eaten the pig food. Then he came to his senses and realised that even his father's servants had more to eat than he did. So, he said to himself he would return home and ask forgiveness from God and his father and ask to be hired as one of his servants. (6)

3 One day the younger of two sons asked his father if he could have his inheritance. The father divided his property and the younger son set off for a distant land. There he spent all his money on having a good time. Because there was a famine, he worked looking after pigs. Then he came to his senses. He returned home and said to his father that he had sinned against heaven and against him. His father forgave him and gave a feast in his honour. (6)

4 The elder son was very angry that a feast had been given for his younger brother. When he returned from work he refused to go into the house. He said to his father that he had worked hard all his life but had never been given a party like this. It was unfair that his brother who had squandered everything should be treated so well. But the father said to him that he had continually enjoyed everything he had; he should celebrate the return of his lost brother. (6)

5 The younger son took his inheritance and then spent it all in a distant land on prostitutes and having a good time. He realised his mistake when he was so hungry he could have eaten pig food. He returned home, saying that he had sinned against God and his father. Meanwhile, the elder son had worked hard, so when he found out his father was giving a party for his brother he was angry and complained to his father that he had never given him a party. (6)

Part c questions:

1 The parable teaches the following about human nature. Firstly, we want to go our own way and be independent, even rebellious, just as the younger son wanted to leave his father's house. Secondly, it shows that when things go wrong, we want to make things right again. Thirdly, it demonstrates that, like the elder son, we want to be appreciated and we get upset and jealous if we feel unfairly treated. (6)

2 Forgiveness is illustrated in two ways. The father forgives his younger son because he is generous and loving. In fact, before the son repents of his sins the father is already waiting to forgive him. So, there is a parallel between the father and God; the father's forgiveness illustrates how God's redemption is for all sinners. Forgiveness is contrasted with the elder son's inability to be generous and failure to rejoice that his brother has repented. (6)

3 The elder brother represents the kind of Pharisee who is so obsessed with keeping God's Law to the letter that he is unable to forgive those who have broken it. They think that 'sinners' – all those who are outside the Law – cannot enter God's kingdom. The elder son's reaction reflects the anger many Pharisees felt about Jesus' teaching, because he taught that the 'lost' of Israel would be the first to enter the Kingdom of God. This seemed to them very unfair. (6)

4 Sin means disobeying God and separating oneself from Him. In the parable, this is symbolised by the younger son travelling to a foreign land and living a riotous life, and in this way breaking many of God's Commandments. The greatest sin, though, came when he was prepared to live with pigs and even contemplate eating their food because in Judaism pigs are considered unclean and the food would not have been kosher. (6)

5 The younger son's return home represents repentance because repentance means a change of heart and mind. When the son was living with the pigs he realised that as a Jew he had now well and truly placed himself outside God's Law and yet he still had sufficient trust in his father to ask for his forgiveness. His return journey is a symbol of his change of heart. The feast symbolises God's joy for all those who repent. (6)

Part d questions:

1 On the face of it, it seems that the father did not act fairly. His younger son had taken his share of his inheritance and spent it all. When he came back, he was forgiven and his return was publicly celebrated. The elder brother meanwhile had worked hard and not received any reward. The father did not treat his two sons fairly.

On the other hand, the father made everything on the farm available for his elder son's enjoyment. It was not his fault that his son did not take advantage of it. He acted out of mercy when his younger son returned penniless and starving, as any father would. He would have been less than human if he had acted 'fairly' and sent his younger son away.

Therefore, in one way the statement is true and the father did act unfairly, but the story is not about fairness; it is about mercy and forgiveness. (7)

2 Deliberately behaving badly is never acceptable. If a person deliberately causes harm to another person by intentionally breaking any of the Ten Commandments, for example, the action could never be justified. Furthermore, if the person thinks they can later say they are sorry and be forgiven, then it is obvious they can't really mean they are sorry.

On the other hand, many of us do bad things unintentionally or without fully thinking through the consequences of our action. We might be led on by peer pressure, or be misled because we don't know all the facts about the situation. Later we might realise that what we have done was bad. It is then when we say we are sorry that we hope to be forgiven.

In conclusion, I don't think the statement is at all right. An intentionally bad action cannot be made good simply by saying sorry. (7)

3 It depends on what is meant by forgiveness. Some might argue that whatever someone has done we should forgive them because they are still a human being, made in the image of God, and it is not for us to judge them. Also, the person who forgives is able to get on with their lives; if they don't forgive, hatred can destroy them.

Others argue that forgiveness doesn't mean a person should go unpunished. If someone has been very wicked and carried out cold-blooded murder, for example, then at the very least they should be imprisoned for life. To quote the phrase: 'we must love the sinner but not the sin'. The culprit and society need to feel that the harm caused by the crime has been paid off – which could even include the death penalty.

So, I think we should forgive people no matter what they have done. But they may still need to be punished for their bad actions. (7)

4 No one knows us better than we know ourselves. We have a conscience and although we may choose to ignore it, sooner or later the sense of guilt becomes very clear. Dietrich Bonhoeffer, for example, went to the USA during the rise of Nazism but his conscience told him that he should return to Germany to help overthrow Hitler, even though his friends tried to persuade him to stay in America.

On the other hand, Jesus told a parable in which he said it was easy to see the speck of dust in your neighbour's eye and fail to see the plank in one's own. He meant that we frequently fail to see our own faults even though they are obvious to others. This is because it is often difficult to see ourselves as others view us.

I think it is easier to see our own faults than to see them in others, but we have to give ourselves time to reflect and listen to our conscience. (7)

5 From the perspective of the elder son he could rightly feel very annoyed that his younger brother had broken almost every rule that a pious Jew should have kept to. He had dishonoured his father by squandering his money. He had mixed with bad company and slept with prostitutes. He had eaten non-kosher food and lived with pigs. His father's reaction was far too generous and must have made the elder brother feel left out and unappreciated. He had very good reasons not to forgive his brother.

But from another perspective, as a good Jew, he should know that God says that He wants 'mercy not sacrifice'. In other words, being religious by keeping to the rituals is not enough. A family functions when its members are generous and merciful to each other. So, the brother should learn to be more grown up and swallow his pride and forgive.

So, I don't think the elder son was right. I can see why he was angry, but as the older person he should have been more mature and behaved like his father. (7)

2.8 The Sower

Part a questions:

1 A parable is a story or saying that compares the Kingdom of God with everyday human events. (2)

2 Persecution is harassment or ill-treatment on grounds of religious beliefs. (2)

3 The seed represents God's word. (2)

4 Faith is having an active trust in someone or in God. (2)

5 A disciple is a follower or student. (2)

Part b questions:

1 A farmer went out to sow. As he sowed, some seed fell on the path and the birds ate it up. Some seed fell on rocky ground where the soil was thin and it grew but, as it had no roots, it died because of lack of moisture. Some seed fell among the thistles, which soon choked it. Other seeds fell on good ground and these bore a hundred times more than was sown. (6)

2 Jesus said the seed was the word of God. The path represents those who do not believe in God's word because of evil. The rock represents those who believe with joy but lack stamina and give up. The thorns are those whose faith is choked by their desire for money and life's worries. The good ground represents those who have good and noble hearts, and who live by the word. (6)

3 The seed the farmer sowed fell onto all sorts of different ground. The seed that fell on the path was trampled on and eaten by birds. The seed that fell on rock died because it had no moisture. The seed that fell on the ground with thistles was soon choked by them. The seed that fell on good ground grew up and multiplied a hundred times. (6)

4 The seed that fell on rocky ground grew up but then died because of lack of moisture. Jesus said this is like people who receive the word of God with joy but who lack stamina and give up when life gets difficult. The seed that fell on thorny ground grew up but was then choked by the thistles. Jesus said this was like people who hear God's word but then the cares of the world and love of money choke their faith and they give up. (6)

Part c questions:

1 The parable teaches that not everyone will receive Jesus' teaching in the same way. There are people for whom teaching on the Kingdom of God means nothing – like the seed on the path. Others might be disciples for a while but when they are questioned or challenged about their faith they give up. For others, being a disciple is attractive but not when it comes to making sacrifices – their faith is replaced by wanting wealth and fame. Others do become good disciples and their lives are transformed. (6)

2 Jesus had to explain the parable to his disciples because quite often they did not fully understand who Jesus was or what his teaching about the Kingdom of God was about. Jesus wanted to make sure that when the disciples went off to preach the Good News by themselves they would really understand what this parable was all about. As he said, if they could understand this parable, then they would understand all the parables. (6)

3 The seeds that fell on the path were eaten by birds. The seed represents the word of God or Jesus' teaching about the Good News of the Kingdom of God. The path symbolises those

people who completely reject the Good News because, according to Jesus' explanation, the devil makes them disbelieve. The good soil, though, represents those people who are open to God's word and have 'good and noble hearts'. Their lives are changed. (6)

4   Jesus assumed that everyone has some understanding about growing plants. Therefore he used the story of the different soils to explain how people respond to his teaching about the Kingdom of God. Some reject it completely (the compacted soil of the path). The thin soil is the person who only has superficial faith. The soil among the thorns is the person who prefers worldly goods and the good soil is the person who has complete faith and is transformed by the Good News. (6)

5   The Kingdom of God is God's presence in the world and in our lives now, not just in the future. The parable teaches that not everyone is prepared to receive the Good News of the Kingdom because it requires effort and it means changing how one lives. Some reject it completely. Some like the idea but they lack stamina and others prefer the material luxuries of this world and are not prepared to sacrifice them. Finally, those who do make the effort find the Kingdom transforms their lives. (6)

Part d questions:

1   Genuine faith is not easy to define. If it means never questioning one's belief in God, then it would be very hard to imagine how it could be achieved. Even Jesus questioned God's will in the Garden of Gethsemane. Everyone has their doubts and I can imagine that even great people of faith such as Martin Luther King must have wondered whether what he was doing was right when people were harmed or killed while protesting for their civil rights.

On the other hand, if by genuine faith we mean the faith of people who commit their lives to a cause that they believe is their Christian duty then there are many people with genuine faith. In fact, if they have doubts, their faith is all the more impressive. Examples of people with this genuine faith are Trevor Huddleston and Dietrich Bonhoeffer, who both stood up against injustice and evil.

I don't think Jesus ever said no one has genuine faith in God because he said in his Parable of the Sower that some people's faith grew a hundred per cent and we have examples of those kinds of people today. (7)

2   Judging by the popularity of the tele-evangelists in the USA and the growing number of charismatic churches in the UK, there is certainly a form of Christianity to which people are attracted because it offers them good fortune now. Good fortune might be in the form of healing miracles, or success in business or acquiring new friends.

But this is not the only kind of religion to which people are attracted. Others want a religion that offers them a means of reflecting on the deeper questions of life. They want to develop their moral values and come to know God better in their daily lives. They don't seek good fortune because fortune is a form of luck that is separate from God.

In conclusion I agree with this statement because even though those who don't think religion is about good fortune in material terms still want God to make their lives better. (7)

3   At its most basic, Jesus' teaching on the Kingdom of God asks his followers to love God and to love their neighbour. This may be demanding but it is not unrealistic. There are plenty of examples in the Gospels where this happens. For example, the sinful woman who anoints Jesus' feet shows her love and devotion even though she is despised by society.

On the other hand, Jesus asks anyone who wants to enter the Kingdom to give up their money and to leave their families. He says a follower must be prepared to suffer, even to die.

These are unrealistic demands as money is needed to live and leaving one's family breaks the Commandment to honour one's parents or be loyal to one's wife or husband.

I don't think the Kingdom does make unrealistic demands on people. It makes great demands and it may be the case that a particular person may suffer or die for the Kingdom, but this is not so for all followers. (7)

4 Lots of people do switch off when they hear about religion. This may be because they are persuaded by people like Richard Dawkins that religion is dangerous and fanatical and also because they consider that science has shown that religious views of the world are wrong. Many find religious worship boring and irrelevant.

On the other hand, there are more people in the world who have a religious faith than those who don't. Millions of people find a religious faith gives a sense of meaning to their lives that science alone cannot do. Furthermore, far from turning people off, religion inspires them to create great art, music and architecture.

In conclusion, it is a fact that not everyone is turned off by religion. It may be the case that our culture and society is not very religious, but millions of people find religion essential in their lives. (7)

5 It would be very odd if Jesus' teaching about the Kingdom of God was about failure. His teaching is about the success of the Kingdom and how it can transform society and personal lives. For example, the ending of the Parable of the Sower is about how God's word creates people with 'good and noble hearts'. It is a story that is designed to encourage people to persevere and flourish.

However, most of the parable is really about coping with failure. The people represented by the path, rocky ground and thorns all fail to meet the demands of the Kingdom and they either reject it or give up. Jesus told the parable so that his disciples would have a realistic view when preaching and not become depressed when it failed.

So, I think that while it is true that Jesus told the parable so that his disciples would be realistic and cope with failure, it was also designed to encourage them to persevere. (7)

Theme 2: Jesus' life, death and resurrection

2.9 The birth of Jesus

Part a questions:

1 Joseph was engaged to marry Mary. (2)

2 Mary was the mother of Jesus. (2)

3 A miracle is an act of God that breaks the laws of physics. (2)

4 Christ means anointed one. (2)

5 Faith means having an active trust in someone or in God. (2)

Part b questions:

1 Mary was engaged to be married to Joseph when she found she was pregnant because of the Holy Spirit. Joseph could have broken off the engagement and disgraced her but an angel appeared to him in a dream and encouraged him to marry Mary. The angel also told him that their son should be called Jesus. When Mary gave birth, they called the baby Jesus. (6)

2   Joseph was engaged to marry Mary but then he found out that she was pregnant. Joseph was a righteous man and wanted to break off the engagement quietly. It was then that an angel appeared to Joseph in a dream and told him not to leave Mary but to marry her. The angel also told him to call the child Jesus because he would save the people from their sins.   (6)

3   When Joseph discovered Mary was expecting a baby he decided that as a kind and righteous person he ought to break off the engagement quietly and out of the public eye. He didn't want her to be disgraced. While he was thinking about doing this, an angel of the Lord appeared to him in a dream and told him not to leave her but instead to marry her. The angel told Joseph that he was to name their child Jesus. Joseph did as the angel told him.   (6)

4   The angel was God's messenger and appeared to Joseph in a dream. Joseph had found out that Mary was pregnant. Even though they were engaged to be married Joseph was deciding whether to break off their engagement privately to save her any humiliation. The angel told Joseph not to do this but to marry her and call their son Jesus. The angel's role was to make sure the prophecy of Isaiah, that a virgin would give birth to a son, was fulfilled.   (6)

5   Joseph was engaged to be married to Mary. He then found out that she was pregnant and decided that probably the best thing to do was to break off the engagement. However, he was a good and righteous person so he didn't want to make a public fuss, because this would mean Mary would be disgraced. Instead, he decided to do the whole thing quietly and discretely. However, he changed his mind after he was visited by God's angel and instead married Mary.   (6)

Part c questions:

1   Joseph is important because his character and faith are tested in a different manner from the way that Mary is tested. He is probably much older than she is and married her to look after his children. Then he finds she is pregnant, but not by him. As a good Jew he knows he can break off the engagement and being a good man he decides to do this quietly so as not to disgrace Mary. But he then has to obey the angel and be obedient to God's will even though it could have brought great shame on him.   (6)

2   Jesus' birth is understood by Matthew to be the fulfilment of many Old Testament prophecies. The name Jesus in Hebrew is Joshua. Joshua means 'God who saves people' – just as Joshua in the Old Testament had saved the children of Israel by leading them into the promised land. So, when the angel tells Joseph that their son is called Jesus, this is because he will save people from their sins and lead them to the Kingdom of God.   (6)

3   The story shows that God is personal and makes Himself known in various ways to humans. Dreams and angels in the ancient world were well known as a means by which God could communicate His intentions. These show how God is directly concerned with humans because He cares and loves them. For example, God directly instructs Joseph not to leave Mary so that He can carry out His greatest act of love, which is to become human Himself. (6)

4   Firstly, the importance of Mary is she is to fulfil Isaiah's prophecy that a young girl would have a child whose name is Immanuel, which means 'God is with us'. Secondly, that as a young pregnant girl she knew that she would have to be brave. The story tells how Joseph almost divorced her when he found she was pregnant. Finally, she must have had great trust and faith in God that her unusual pregnancy would turn out for the good.   (6)

Part d questions:

1 Many people would agree that we have lost the true meaning of Christmas and become obsessed with parties and buying expensive presents. People are not interested in the deeper religious reasons for the festival; they just want to have fun and are content to enjoy it at a superficial level.

However, others would argue that Christmas is one of the few events that people do understand. Churches are often full on Christmas Eve and Christmas Day, schools put on nativity plays and the news of Jesus' birth is in shops and newspapers. People make an effort to be kind to each other and to give to charities. All this suggests that people know how to enter into the spirit of Christmas.

Therefore I think that while there is some truth in the statement, a lot of people understand that Christmas is a time of giving and so I don't think society has forgotten the meaning of Christmas. (7)

2 The story of Jesus' birth does tell us a lot about God's love. God is prepared to become a human and be born to a girl who isn't yet married and who Joseph must have thought had committed adultery. This shows how God's love for humanity is not proud and doesn't discriminate against people because of their gender or social class.

On the other hand, Jesus' death on the cross as God's son shows even more clearly how he was prepared to take on the sins of the world and sacrifice himself on our behalf. Jesus himself said that there is no greater sign of love than laying down one's life for a friend.

I think that Jesus' death tells us more about God's love than his birth. That is because sacrificing your own life for another person is the most unselfish act a person can do for another and so this illustrates God's love for us more than anything else. (7)

3 Children should have the same rights as adults because they rely on adults for their existence. Children depend on adults for their protection, food and clothes and education. As rights are there to uphold human dignity, it is reasonable for society to give children these rights and have organisations such as UNICEF to make sure they are kept to.

On the other hand, human rights imply responsibilities. If children had the same rights as adults then they would have to be held responsible if they committed a crime or if they made a racist comment in public. This is clearly wrong as children are not yet old enough to understand what they are doing.

Therefore, to conclude, children should have rights, but these cannot be exactly the same as adult rights – in fact, they should have some rights that are not available to adults, such as the right to a parent. (7)

4 Some argue that Mary is the heroine of the story of Jesus' birth. After all, she had a lot to lose by becoming pregnant. She was engaged to Joseph, which was almost the same as being married, and so when she found she was pregnant she knew that not only might he leave her but she would then be despised by the rest of society. So she had to be brave and trusting.

Others argue that Joseph is the real hero of the story. It is likely that he had children already and married Mary to look after them and himself. He was a very respectable man and lived according to the Jewish Law. Not leaving Mary, even though he was entitled to, meant that he was prepared to look after her and a child who was not his own, in the face of society's ridicule.

However, I think Mary was the real heroine of the story because she would have had to face much greater social criticisms as a young pregnant girl than Joseph. (7)

5 The only reason that the birth of Jesus is significant is if Mary was a virgin when she gave birth to Jesus. If she was, then it is a miracle and shows that Jesus is God's son. However, a lot of people think that the Old Testament passage that Matthew quotes just means Mary was a young girl whose child would be called Immanuel. If that is so, then the story of Jesus' birth is just preparing us to see how he was the Messiah who would later go on to teach.

On the other hand, it is clear that Matthew quotes Isaiah because he wants to show that Mary is the young girl of the prophecy and her pregnancy is caused by God. Jesus is therefore God's son. If he had not been God's son, then Jesus' teaching would not have had authority and would not have challenged the Jewish leaders and their teaching.

So, I don't think the birth of Jesus is as important as his teaching. I think it is intended to show Jesus' place in Judaism, but what really matters is his teaching. (7)

2.10 The temptations

Part a questions:

1 Temptation is the desire to do something wrong. (2)

2 Worship is giving God praise and honour. (2)

3 Fasting is going without food to enable oneself to be more aware of God. (2)

4 'Son of God' is the term used to describe Jesus' unique relationship with God. (2)

5 Jesus fasted for 40 days and 40 nights. (2)

Part b questions:

1 When the devil tempted Jesus to turn stones into bread, Jesus told him that the scripture says 'humans cannot live on bread alone.' When the devil offered him the kingdoms of the world if he would bow down to him, Jesus said that the scripture says 'worship the Lord your God and serve only him.' Finally, when the devil tempted him to jump from the top of the temple, Jesus replied that the scripture says 'Do not put the Lord your God to the test.' (6)

2 The devil took Jesus to a very high mountain and showed him all the kingdoms of the world and their power. He said to Jesus that he could have all these if he would bow down and worship him. Jesus said to him, 'Be off, Satan. It is written in the law that you shall worship and serve only God.' (6)

3 Jesus had been in the wilderness for 40 days and nights. Then the devil appeared. First he said that if Jesus was really the Son of God he could command stones into bread. Then he took him to the Temple and he said to him that if he were to jump off then God's angels would stop him falling. Then the devil took him to a high place and showed him all the kingdoms of the world and said he could have these if he worshipped him. (6)

4 Jesus had been fasting for 40 days and 40 nights in the wilderness. He was very hungry when Satan appeared and said to him. 'If you are the Son of God, turn these stones into bread.' Jesus replied that it is written that people do not live on bread alone. They live on God's words. (6)

5   To the first temptation Jesus replied by quoting Scripture that people do not live on bread alone but by God's words. To the second temptation Jesus replied that in the Bible it says that no one should put God to the test. To the third temptation Jesus answered that it was written that only God could be worshipped. (6)

Part c questions:

1   Having been baptised, Jesus may have felt that his calling to carry out God's will was easy. The temptations are powerful reminders of how easy it would be to misuse his gifts for his own glory and power and not for God's. If he had fed all the poor he would have become a great political leader. He could have ruled a mighty kingdom. He could have been seen as a super-hero with magical powers. All these temptations test his vocation. (6)

2   The temptations teach that firstly he is God's son. This is because even the devil assumes he must have God's powers to do miraculous deeds. Secondly, they teach that as God's son he must be completely obedient to His will, not to his own. By resisting the thought that he could become rich and powerful, Jesus knows that his relationship with God is one of sacrifice and love. Only God is to be worshipped. (6)

3   Jesus resisted temptation because in his own prayer he taught 'lead us not into temptation'. Jesus was tempted like anyone else because he was human and as God's son he could have misused his powers for his own glory and political power. Jesus' example is to teach all those with power how to use it for the good of others. Jesus resisted temptation as an example to his followers of his genuine obedience to God. (6)

4   In the Ten Commandments it is stated that only God may be worshipped. Worship of any other gods or people is blasphemy and idolatry. This is because God is supreme, and anything less than God would not be worthy of our complete obedience and love. Jesus is therefore warning against worshipping political leaders or giving too much power to any human being. Jesus' own obedience to God, for example, led to his crucifixion. (6)

5   It would have been easy for Jesus to feed the poor miraculously, but he knew that his teaching was more important than physical food. This temptation also is a reminder of the time in the wilderness when God sent Moses bread from heaven. This was also a test because he was told only to eat what was needed each day. The test is even greater here because Jesus is fasting as a sign of true obedience to God's will. (6)

Part d questions:

1   Many people believe that unfairness should always be stopped even if it means using violence to achieve it. In South Africa the apartheid system was very unfair. The ANC led by Nelson Mandela often used violence to try to change the government's mind. Eventually they achieved equality for black Africans and this was a very good thing. Most people thought that violence was justified.

On the other hand, others say that violence is wrong even if it brings about something good. Innocent people get killed and in the end things are only changed because force was used. In America, where there was similar racial injustice, Martin Luther King campaigned without violence and eventually won equality for black Americans.

I consider that the statement is correct. It is tempting to use violence and sometimes people do when faced with unfair situations, but it is not the right way. (7)

2   It is only bad people who are tempted and then act. That is because they lack the willpower to resist doing wrong and even though their conscience may tell them otherwise, they haven't got the strength of character to resist. Jesus describes this kind of person in the Parable of the Sower when the seed lands on rocky ground. Bad people such as Harold Shipman gave in to temptation by using their power for themselves.

On the other hand, good people may also be tempted but choose to resist. Some argue that it is a greater sign of goodness to resist doing bad things than never to have been in a situation of having to choose. Oscar Romero, for example, could have lived a comfortable life, but he chose to stand up for the poor, even though this cost him his life.

In conclusion, I disagree with the statement. Good people are tempted and it is a sign of their true goodness that they resist. (7)

3   Although soldiers are trained not to give away information under torture, there comes a point where even the strongest person weakens and breaks down. This is also true for less extreme temptations. In Christian teaching, the cause of human weakness of this kind is original sin. Humans may wish to do good but they are also naturally rebellious, selfish and weak-willed. It is not even theoretically possible to resist all temptation.

However, people can and do resist temptation. For example, there are many who have given up smoking or drinking too much. People learn to know their weaknesses and train themselves to overcome them. Furthermore, there is no 'original sin' caused by the Fall of Adam and Eve; humans are neither good nor bad but choose freely what they think is good.

I don't think it is always possible to resist temptation because humans are weak-willed and affected by sin. This is why life is a struggle and it is this struggle that makes us better people. (7)

4   Many argue that the end does not justify the means for two reasons. First, it is impossible to know what the effects are of any of our actions. For example, if I lie to protect a friend of mine and later he is found out, then I could find myself in a lot of trouble. Second, there are some things that are just wrong. For example, torture is against the UN Declaration of Human Rights because it is demeaning to treat any human being as an object, even to achieve good in the end.

However, others argue that sometimes we have to do things that are unpleasant for the greater good. So, torturing a terrorist to get out of him information that would save a hundred innocent people is justified by saving many lives.

In conclusion, I agree that the ends justify the means, but only where there is clearly more good achieved than bad. (7)

5   If morality is about making the greatest number of people happy at any one moment and cheating makes me happy (e.g. it allows me to pass my physics test) and no one is disadvantaged by it, then there can be nothing wrong with it. If I don't believe in God, then there is no reason why I should have a guilty conscience as there is no God judging me, and if conscience is just my upbringing I can easily dismiss it.

However, there are some things that are immoral, whether or not anyone knows about them and even if no one is directly harmed. For example, suppose I commit adultery and no one knows except the person with whom I have the affair; this makes me a less honest person and one who is prepared to break my promises. Cheating alters the kind of person I am.

I agree with the statement. What matters is that no one is hurt by what we do and although we can't always know if we have hurt people, cheating, in theory, is not wrong. (7)

Part a questions:

1 A disciple is a follower or student. (2)

2 A miracle is an act of God that breaks the laws of physics. (2)

3 Simon Peter was a fisherman and became Jesus' most important disciple. (2)

4 Sin is disobeying God and separating oneself from Him. (2)

5 Faith is having an active trust in someone or in God. (2)

Part b questions:

1 After the catch of fish Simon Peter fell to his knees and said that he was a sinner. This was because he realised that Jesus was no ordinary person and he felt that Jesus was holy and he shouldn't be near him. Jesus told him not to be afraid because he was now going to 'catch' people not fish. Then Peter left everything and followed him. (6)

2 Jesus had been preaching from Simon Peter's boat. When he was finished he told Peter to go to the deep waters and let down his nets. Peter said they had been fishing all night and caught nothing so far. However, he did as Jesus had told him and let down his net. He then found the net was so full of fish that the other fishermen went over and also filled their boat with fish. (6)

3 Jesus told Simon Peter to row out into the lake so he could address the crowd. When he had finished he told Peter to go out to the deep waters and let down his nets. Even though Peter said they would catch nothing, amazingly his net was full of fish. Peter said he was not worthy to be a disciple but Jesus told him and the others that they would now fish for people. The disciples left everything and followed him. (6)

4 Jesus called the first disciples by telling Simon Peter to row out to the deep waters and put down his nets. Peter said they had been fishing all night and caught nothing. However, when he brought in his nets he found they were completely full of fish. Peter was overcome and said that he was not worthy to follow Jesus. But Jesus said to him and to James and John that from now on they would 'catch men'. They left everything and followed him. (6)

5 After Jesus got into Simon Peter's boat he first preached to the crowd and then he told Peter to drop his nets into the deep waters. Peter was doubtful as they had caught nothing all night. But he did as he was told and caught a huge amount of fish. Peter said to Jesus he was not worthy to follow him, but Jesus told him not to be afraid because from now on they would be catching people not fish. (6)

Part c questions:

1 The story teaches that Jesus has power over nature. The disciples have caught very few fish and then on Jesus' command they find so many that their nets are breaking. It might also teach that Jesus has very special knowledge – perhaps this is to indicate that as God's son he is omniscient. The story teaches that Jesus has compassion and cares for his disciples because he helps them and stops them going hungry. (6)

2 Simon Peter was a fisherman on the Sea of Galilee and that is how he made his living. Now Jesus is asking him to use his skills to bring people to understand the Good News of the Kingdom of God. He has just filled his boat to overflowing with fish, which he now

understands is a symbol of the abundant joy that the Kingdom of God offers. His role now is to teach and preach about God's Kingdom. (6)

3 The call teaches that to be a good disciple requires faith. The story draws a contrast between Simon Peter's lack of faith and the faith of the large crowds who have listened to Jesus. Discipleship also requires obedience and trust. Peter is not certain that Jesus is right but he is willing to carry out his wishes. Finally, Peter's confession illustrates that a disciple must be humble and admit his faults. (6)

4 Simon Peter's reaction to the great catch of fish is to contrast his character before and after the miracle. Beforehand Peter is a slightly arrogant and mistrusting person. When Jesus tells him to go into the deep waters Peter thinks he knows better as he is the fisherman. Afterwards, though, Peter is full of remorse. He admits his faults and becomes humble. The miracle illustrates the qualities that a good disciple needs. (6)

5 The Kingdom of God firstly demands that a person is humble. Simon Peter was humbled by the miracle of the catch of fish and realised that he had been arrogant to question Jesus' advice. The Kingdom demands sacrifice. Jesus says to the disciples that they are now to become fishers of people and that means giving up their lives as fishermen to preach the Good News. (6)

Part d questions:

1 Faith means having complete certainty about something even if this cannot be proved. If as a mountaineer I have faith in the rope that is stopping me from falling, that means I can climb the mountain. If I didn't have faith in it then I would never be able to scale the rocks. In the same way, some people think that having faith in God means never doubting, because if one did, then His existence would make no sense.

On the other hand, in the example of the rope, the mountaineer has tested his rope and made sure that it works. It would be very difficult to have faith in something merely because someone else tells me it is true. Most of us have to have good reasons for believing, and having faith in God is no different.

So, that is why I disagree with the statement. Blind faith is not real faith; doubting one's faith in God is part of coming to a full understanding of His existence. (7)

2 Dietrich Bonhoeffer gave up his career as a university lecturer in the USA because his Christian faith told him that to stay and teach was not facing up to his duty to return to Germany to face Hitler and resist evil. It was a wise decision because although it was in his own words 'the terrible alternative', if he had stayed his guilty conscience would have made his life a misery. In the end, his decision cost him his life.

On the other hand, some argue that faith is irrational and cannot be a good guide. Bonhoeffer's decision wasn't wise because he could have done far more good teaching at university. In some ways, what he did was quite selfish because it was done to ease his conscience. The same could be said of Jesus' disciples when they gave up their careers as fishermen to follow him.

I don't think it is wise to give up everything for faith. Faith needs to be guided by reason, otherwise actions could be irrational and selfish. (7)

3 Some people argue that any religion that forces a person to leave their family behind is a false one. This is because it is your family that has nurtured you and it is a basic duty, as stated in the Ten Commandments, to honour your mother and father. The disciples weren't wrong to follow Jesus, providing they also continued to support their wives, children and parents.

But some people argue that there are times when there are greater duties to perform. For example, during war, fighting for your country is more important than staying at home. James Mawdsley is an example of a young man who felt that his Christian duty was to campaign for human rights in Burma, even though this meant leaving his family and being imprisoned for years.

I think the situation decides which duties one should obey. There are times when duty to family is less important, so the disciples were not necessarily wrong to leave their families and follow Jesus. (7)

4   For some, wealth is a barrier to faith. They think that as faith requires leaving wealth and material things behind then they would rather have the certainty of wealth than the uncertainty of faith. Some argue that as we only have one life, then to waste it on beliefs that cannot be proved is foolish.

However, for others, having faith in God is a way of making sense of life and a framework of values to live by. Having wealth is neither a good nor a bad thing; what matters is how it is used. From a Christian position, wealth gives a person the opportunity to give to charity and help those less well off than themselves.

In conclusion, I think wealth can be a barrier to faith. Christian teaching frequently calls on people to make large material sacrifices for God and I think these are unrealistic. (7)

5   On the one hand, it makes much more sense to see the catch of fish as a parable. If it is not treated as a parable, it then looks more like a magic trick and the symbolism of the story is lost. As a parable, it is a story about how many people Simon Peter and the others will convert to Christianity. It is also a story about the abundant joy the Kingdom of God will bring to the world.

On the other hand, if this didn't happen, then Peter wouldn't have fallen to his knees and asked Jesus for forgiveness. As a miracle, it was intended to teach Peter who Jesus was, as well as giving him a sense of the power of God's Kingdom.

As I think miracles are possible, then I think the catch of fish did happen and it is not just a parable. Of course, it is also meant to teach, just as a parable does. (7)

2.12 Peter's declaration

Part a questions:

1   Christ means the anointed one. (2)

2   John the Baptist was the person who baptised Jesus. (2)

3   Peter was one of Jesus' closest disciples. (2)

4   'Son of Man' is the term used to describe Jesus' role as the one who would suffer for others. (2)

5   A prophet is a person chosen by God to speak God's message to the people. (2)

Part b questions:

1   After Peter declared Jesus was the Messiah, Jesus warned them not to say anything to anyone about him. Jesus then said, as Son of Man, he would suffer many things, he would be rejected by the Jewish authorities and rise again. Peter said he would not let Jesus do this. Jesus turned

on Peter and told him not to tempt him. He said to him, 'Get behind me, Satan. You are thinking in human terms not as God wishes.' (6)

2 Jesus asked the disciples who the people thought he was. They replied that some thought he was John the Baptist, some that he was Elijah and others a prophet. He asked them who they thought he was. Peter answered, 'the Messiah'. Jesus said that as the Son of Man he would have to suffer, be killed and then rise again. When Peter said they wouldn't let this happen, Jesus told him that he was being tempted by Satan. (6)

3 As Jesus and his disciples were near Caesarea Philippi Jesus asked them who the people thought he was. The disciples answered that some thought he was John the Baptist, some Elijah and others a prophet. Jesus asked them who they thought he was. Peter said Jesus was the Messiah. Jesus told them not to tell anyone and that he would suffer, die and then rise again. Peter told him off. Jesus rebuked him saying, 'Get behind me, Satan.' (6)

4 As they were on their way to Caesarea Philippi, Jesus asked the disciples who the people thought he was. They answered that some were saying he was John the Baptist, others that he was Elijah and others one of the prophets. Then Jesus asked them who they thought he was. Peter replied, 'You are the Messiah.' (6)

Part c questions:

1 Jesus might have used the term 'Son of Man' because he saw himself as a representative of mankind. Perhaps he thought that his death as a martyr would mean that the things he stood for – justice, mercy and love for ordinary people – would become public. In the Old Testament Isaiah spoke of a suffering servant who was killed because society rejected him and when this happened they became guilty and realised how sinfully they had behaved. (6)

2 In Judaism, Messiah meant God's anointed one. This typically referred to a king or military leader who would bring peace and justice using force or great miracles. But Jesus taught that the Messiah would not be a military leader but a suffering servant who would die and bring in a very different kind of kingdom. He did not conform to expectations. (6)

3 Jesus had just explained that as Messiah he was going to suffer many things. In Jewish thought, the Messiah, as God's anointed one, would not establish God's kingdom on earth through suffering but by performing great miracles and using force to get rid of Israel's enemies. Peter must have been disappointed and that is why he said he would not let Jesus suffer. But Jesus saw Peter tempting him like Satan had done, so that is why he told him to 'get behind' him. (6)

4 Peter probably meant that Jesus was the Messiah or anointed one who would, according to popular Jewish thought, be a leader who would establish God's kingdom on earth. People looked forward to a time when a descendent of King David would establish peace and justice by ridding Israel of her enemies. This explains why Peter was disappointed when Jesus said he was going to suffer and why he told Jesus that they would not let this happen to him. (6)

5 In the Old Testament Elijah had been a very great prophet. He had led the people to worship God and reject idolatry. Many hoped he would return and prepare the people for God's Kingdom. That is why some thought that Elijah's spirit must be living on in Jesus. In the same way, many considered John the Baptist as a popular prophet and as he had just died, they thought his spirit must be living on in Jesus. (6)

Part d questions:

1 Living a good life is really all that matters. If that means being kind to people, keeping to the laws of society and being a good citizen, it cannot really make any difference whether you believe in God or not. In fact, some people who believe in God do very bad things – they cause holy wars or become suicide bombers or look down on non-believers.

On the other hand, believing in God should mean that a person takes their duties to others all the more seriously. Someone who does not believe in God may not think that it matters too much whether you keep to your promises or not. But for the sincere believer, breaking God's commands means that you have broken God's trust as well as the trust of another person.

I conclude that believing in God does make a difference as this ensures that one does truly live a good life. (7)

2 This question depends on what is meant by the term 'messiah'. It could be taken in a general sense of meaning God's chosen one. King David was a messiah because like all kings he was chosen or anointed by God. Jesus clearly wasn't a king in that sense, but he was a very popular figure, as can been seen when he fed 5000 people. As Jesus was careful to avoid being seen as a popular messiah, it matters if he was not the Messiah.

On the other hand, if Messiah means that Jesus was God's son, then it does matter. This would mean that his teaching, death and resurrection have great significance. As God's anointed one, Jesus saw himself as God's suffering servant who would take away the sins of the world.

In conclusion, it matters whether Jesus was the Messiah if this means he was God's son and it also matters if he was not the Messiah in the popular sense. (7)

3 Some argue that giving up something we value for something else makes us value it even more. It is the same when we have to wait to buy a new item for a hobby or we have to save up to buy a piece of furniture for the house. If we get something too easily and without effort then we value it less.

On the other hand, it doesn't follow that the most important things require the biggest sacrifices. For example, getting married might be considered an 'important thing' but if two people are in love then the sacrifices they make in order to be with each other appear very small.

In conclusion, I don't think there is an equation that says the bigger the sacrifice the more something is worth. (7)

4 Many argue that if Jesus had not been God's son, then his death on the cross would have just been a very sad end to a good man and Jesus' resurrection would just be a happy ending to an unhappy story. As it is, it matters a great deal that Jesus as God's son died for the sins of the world and his resurrection therefore is a sign of hope that followed.

However, others think that what really makes Jesus significant is consistency between what he taught and what he did. He argued for justice for the poor and the outcast and was prepared to eat with them, touch and heal them. He argued against the petty religious laws of the Pharisees and was prepared to break them. He was ultimately prepared to die for what he believed in.

In conclusion, non-Christians can agree with the whole statement, but for Christians only the second half of the statement is true. (7)

5 If Jesus was more than a good man, what was he? Some argue that he was a prophet. He was a prophet a bit like Isaiah because he spoke out against false religious practices and made people think about their sins. He showed symbolically how the Temple had become corrupted and needed to be cleansed. As a prophet, he was even prepared to die if this meant people would return to God.

However, some argue that seeing Jesus as a prophet is not enough. A prophet is still a human being and Jesus was more than this. For example, although God performed miracles for the prophet Elijah, this was unlike Jesus who carried out his own miracles. This is because he was God's son and had God's authority to do so.

I am not convinced that miracles are possible however, so although I think Jesus was more than a good man, I do not believe he was God's son but rather a great prophet.   (7)

2.13 The Transfiguration

Part a questions:

1 Transfiguration means a change in Jesus' appearance.   (2)

2 'Son of Man' is the term used to describe Jesus' role as the one who would suffer for others.   (2)

3 God gave Moses the Law at Sinai.   (2)

4 Elijah was a prophet in the Old Testament.   (2)

5 He tells the disciples not to tell anyone what they had seen until his resurrection.   (2)

Part b questions:

1 Jesus was taking the three disciples up a high mountain when suddenly his appearance was changed and he became dazzlingly white. With him appeared Moses and Elijah. Peter wanted to build them some tents. Then from the cloud a voice spoke, saying to the disciples, 'This is my Son, listen to him' and then suddenly the vision disappeared and they were alone. Jesus told them to keep this to themselves.   (6)

2 After the appearance of Elijah and Moses, Peter was very confused and suggested they should build three tents, one for each of them, including Jesus. Then a cloud appeared and a voice said, 'This is my Son whom I love. Listen to him.' Suddenly Moses and Elijah disappeared and Jesus was alone with them. On the way down the mountain, Jesus told them not to say anything about what they had seen to anyone.   (6)

3 On their way down the mountain Jesus told the disciples not to say anything about what they had seen. The disciples asked why the teachers of the law said Elijah must first come. Jesus replied that it was in order to restore society, but in fact he had come and society had killed him. Furthermore, as Son of Man he must also suffer and be rejected.   (6)

4 Jesus took Peter, James and John up a high mountain. Suddenly, in front of them he was transfigured. His clothes became dazzling white and Elijah and Moses appeared, talking with Jesus. Peter said, 'Rabbi, it is good that we are here.' He offered to build three shelters for them – he was very confused as to what was going on. Then suddenly a cloud appeared and from it a voice announced that Jesus was his son and they should listen to him.   (6)

5 Jesus took Peter, James and John up a high mountain. His clothes became dazzling white and Elijah and Moses appeared, talking with Jesus. Peter offered to build three shelters for them.

Then a cloud appeared and a voice announced that Jesus was his son and they should listen to him. On the way down Jesus told the disciples not tell anyone what they had seen. They were confused as they were expecting Elijah to have arrived before the messiah. Jesus told them that Elijah had arrived. (6)

Part c questions:

1 In the Old Testament Moses was given the Law at Mount Sinai and he also led the Israelites out of Egypt to freedom. Elijah was one of God's great prophets and spoke against corruption and the worship of false gods. They both appear in the vision because Jesus is now ranked alongside them, but God's voice tells the disciples only to listen to him. This suggests that Jesus' teaching continues in Moses' and Elijah's footsteps but is also the fulfilment of Law and prophecy. (6)

2 Jesus may have told the disciples not to tell anyone what they had seen and heard because he wanted the people to understand his role as a suffering servant. If they were told about his future heavenly state they might not take seriously his teaching about sacrifice and love. He might have thought that the authorities would arrest him immediately for blasphemy by claiming to be greater than Moses and Elijah without any clear evidence. (6)

3 The Transfiguration teaches about Jesus' divine identity as God's son. The disciples have a profoundly spiritual experience in which they realise that Jesus is the fulfilment of the Law God gave to Moses and the prophecy represented by Elijah. This suggests that Jesus will be bringing a new Law and that as John the Baptist carried out the role of Elijah, then Jesus must therefore be the Messiah. (6)

4 In the vision the disciples see the two figures of Moses and Elijah talking to Jesus. They know that Moses represents the Jewish Law and Elijah represents prophecy. So when the disciples are told by God to 'listen' to Jesus because he is His son, they know that Jesus' mission will be to fulfil the Law and prophecy. But, on the way down they learn that Jesus will carry out this mission as a suffering servant. (6)

5 The voice from the cloud is God's because in the Old Testament God's presence in the wilderness was represented as a cloud. The significance of God's voice is that it speaks to the disciples. In the vision, they have just seen Jesus talking with Moses and Elijah, who represent the Law and prophecy. The disciples are told to listen to Jesus as he is God's son and the fulfilment of the Law and prophecy. (6)

Part d questions:

1 Peter might have understood the Transfiguration and still denied knowing Jesus because at the time he betrayed him, Peter was scared and was potentially in danger. Unlike Jesus he did not have a close relationship with God. Anyway, later on he realised his mistake and was filled with remorse.

On the other hand, I don't think Peter did understand the Transfiguration. He offered to build some tents for Moses, Elijah and Jesus when clearly they weren't physically there but part of a powerful vision. Peter often made mistakes, for example at Caesarea Philippi when he said he wouldn't let Jesus suffer.

Therefore it would seem to me that Peter hadn't really understood what the Transfiguration meant about Jesus' relationship to God. Had he done so, Peter would not later have denied knowing Jesus. (7)

2 For many people, experience of God is to be found in the beauty of nature, in the quiet of a magnificent building or in listening to a piece of music. In the Old Testament, Elijah experienced

God as a gentle whisper or small calm voice rather than in whirlwinds and storms. The religious life of monks and nuns is founded on a day of quiet contemplation and peaceful activity.

However, others have experienced God in very different circumstances. Sometimes in war a person's act of bravery or kindness has shown how people have been moved by their experience of God to do good even during times of evil. The story of Maximilian Kolbe, who gave his life to save another man's life in a Nazi concentration camp, has inspired many people to experience God.

In conclusion, if God is all-loving then He can be experienced in all kinds of unexpected ways. Although it seems more likely that people would experience Him in peace and quietness, this need not be the case. (7)

3   Many have interpreted the Transfiguration as a story of the disciples' insight into Jesus' relationship to two other great teachers, Moses and Elijah. Moses and Elijah were leaders in very different ways from each other. Elijah led the people to worship God and not Baal, and Moses led the people from slavery to freedom. Jesus was also a teacher like them but he offered a new teaching based on love.

However, others have interpreted the Transfiguration to be a story of Jesus' divine relationship with God. God calls him His son and he is shown to be greater than Moses and Elijah. Jesus is more than just a teacher. Furthermore, in his lifetime Jesus performed miracles; his death is seen as atonement for sin and he was resurrected.

In conclusion, from a Christian point of view, Jesus must be more than just a teacher. That is the purpose of the story of the Transfiguration. (7)

4   Many consider that beliefs must come before actions, otherwise how would we know what to do? For example, if I believe that keeping promises is morally good then when I am asked to keep a promise I am going to do just that. If I didn't really understand or believe what promises were then I wouldn't know how to behave. In the same way, if I believe in God then I understand what He requires of me.

However, many disagree with this. Believing something is far easier than acting. For example, I might give to charity because I just know it is the right thing to do. I don't have a belief about charity that I then put into action. Furthermore, lots of people say they believe in things, such as not stealing, but then go and do the opposite.

Believing doesn't necessarily lead to action. For example, many people say they believe it is right to help the poor but do nothing about it. This would suggest that beliefs are often confused and not clear. (7)

5   Some argue that the Transfiguration is more important than the Resurrection because it was the moment when the disciples experienced Jesus' divine status during his lifetime. Whether it was a vision or a powerful religious experience, it showed them that he was more than a teacher or prophet and was God's son. The Transfiguration makes much more sense of Jesus' life and death than the Resurrection as it shows us that even as God's son he was prepared to die for others.

On the other hand, without the Resurrection, Jesus' death would have meant failure. The Resurrection, for Christians, is a sign that death is not the end and that there is hope beyond this life. Jesus had predicted that he would be raised after three days, and the Resurrection confirms the truth of his words.

I think the Transfiguration is more important than the Resurrection because it gives us much greater insight into who Jesus was. (7)

2.14 The sentence, Crucifixion and burial

Part a questions:

1 The notice read 'The King of the Jews'. (2)

2 Crucifixion is the Roman death penalty of being nailed to a cross. (2)

3 Barabbas was a murderer and had led several revolts. (2)

4 Pontius Pilate was the Roman governor of Judea. (2)

5 The Sanhedrin was the Jewish ruling council. (2)

6 Atonement means getting back into a right relationship with God. (2)

7 The Sabbath is the Jewish day of rest. (2)

8 Joseph of Arimathea was a member of the Sanhedrin (the Jewish ruling council). (2)

Part b questions:

1 As it was Passover, the crowd asked Pilate to carry out the custom of releasing a prisoner. Pilate asked the crowd whether they wanted him to release Jesus, the King of the Jews. The chief priests stirred up the crowd and they shouted out that they wanted Jesus to be crucified. Pilate asked what crime Jesus had committed, but they still shouted out 'Crucify him!' So, Pilate released Barabbas and had Jesus flogged. (6)

2 The soldiers led Jesus to the Praetorium. There they dressed him in a purple robe and put a crown of thorns on his head. They mocked him, calling out, 'Hail, King of the Jews.' They hit him and spat on him and pretended to worship him. Then they put his clothes back on and led him off to be crucified. (6)

3 The soldiers made Simon of Cyrene carry Jesus' cross to Golgotha. They offered Jesus drugged wine but he refused it. Then the soldiers crucified him and cast lots for his clothes. Above his head on the cross was a sign that read 'The King of the Jews'. Two robbers were crucified next to him. Passers-by taunted him, saying that he could save himself from the cross. Chief priests and lawyers mocked him as well. (6)

4 Jesus was mocked on the cross by passers-by. They said that as he was able to knock down the Temple and rebuild it, he could easily save himself from the cross. Then members of the Sanhedrin said that although he had saved others, he seemed unable to save himself. They challenged him to come down from the cross and prove himself to be the Messiah. Even the robbers being crucified with him insulted him. (6)

5 When Jesus died, the curtain in the Temple tore in two from top to bottom. The soldier standing at the foot of the cross saw how Jesus died and said that he was the Son of God. Joseph of Arimathea got permission from Pilate to take Jesus' body away. Joseph wrapped Jesus in a linen sheet, laid him in a tomb and rolled a huge stone across the entrance. (6)

6 Joseph of Arimathea was a member of the Jewish ruling council, the Sanhedrin, and when Jesus died on the cross he went to Pontius Pilate and asked him whether he could take Jesus' body and bury it. Pilate was surprised but gave him permission. Joseph wrapped the body in a linen cloth and placed him in a tomb just before the Sabbath began. (6)

7 As it was the Preparation day, Joseph of Arimathea asked Pilate if he could take Jesus' body for burial. Pilate was surprised to hear from the centurion that Jesus had already died. He

gave Joseph permission. Joseph wrapped Jesus' body in a linen cloth and placed it in a rock tomb. He rolled a stone across the entrance. Mary Magdalene and Mary the mother of Jesus saw where Jesus was buried. (6)

Part c questions:

1 Christians believe that Jesus' death was a sacrifice. When he died he offered his life as an atonement by taking the sins of the world upon himself. Because of this sacrifice, God will forgive anyone who repents. Jesus' death removed the barrier between human beings and God that the Fall had created. This was seen symbolically when the curtain separating the Holy of Holies from the rest of the Temple tore in two, allowing everyone to come into the presence of God. (6)

2 The Temple curtain divided the Holy of Holies from the rest of the Temple. The only person who could enter the Holy of Holies was the High Priest on the Day of Atonement. So, the curtain symbolised the barrier between God and human beings, which was caused by human sin. When, therefore, the curtain split in two it symbolised how Jesus' death removed this barrier of sin. Jesus' death allows humans to have a new and full relationship with God. (6)

3 One reason why Jesus had to die is that he had become very popular with the people and the Jewish leaders thought they might lose their authority. So, as he claimed to be working as God's son, they accused him of blasphemy, which in the Jewish Law carried the death penalty. Another reason is that the Roman authorities thought Jesus was a political threat as he was claiming to be a king or messiah. They put him to death on grounds of treason. (6)

4 Jesus was taken to Pilate because the High Priest had found Jesus guilty of blasphemy but under Roman law he was not allowed to carry out the death penalty. Pilate was the Roman governor and so Jesus was sent to be tried by him. The Jewish authorities told Pilate that Jesus was a king and a political threat to Rome. Pilate therefore accused Jesus of being 'King of the Jews' and then had him crucified. (6)

5 The centurion said, 'Surely this man was the Son of God'. The centurion was a Roman soldier and would have worshipped many gods, so for him to say that Jesus was the Son of God was a sign that Jesus' death must have affected him very deeply. It is also a sign that Jesus' sacrifice and death was not just for Jews but for all kinds of people, including non-Jews. (6)

6 Jesus' burial is important because it means that he did actually die. Joseph of Arimathea was a senior Jewish official and he must have had a lot of respect for Jesus to be prepared to place him in his family tomb. He is therefore a reliable witness that Jesus had actually died. This means that when the women arrived at the tomb later they would have expected the body to be there. All these things point to the fact that the Resurrection actually happened. (6)

7 Joseph of Arimathea was a senior Jewish official and a member of the Sanhedrin. The Sanhedrin was responsible for trying Jesus on the charge of blasphemy. The fact that Joseph was prepared to give Jesus a place in the family tomb shows that he must have had a lot of respect for him. It also suggests that not all the Sanhedrin thought Jesus was guilty and deserved to die. (6)

8 There are several reasons why the stone across the door of the tomb was significant. Firstly, it was the custom to seal a tomb because of tomb robbers. This detail is to emphasise that Jesus' body was not stolen but was resurrected. Secondly, sealing the tomb with the stone also shows that the person was really dead. Jesus wasn't in a coma or deep sleep from which he later awoke. The stone shows that his Resurrection actually happened. (6)

Part d questions:

1 Pilate knew that Jesus was innocent of the charges that the chief priests had brought before him. He tried to provoke Jesus into rescuing himself from the situation by asking him about his kingship. He suggested that the crowd should request Jesus' release as was his custom every year at Passover. In spite of this, he still ordered his execution. This is weak behaviour because he had the power to set him free but he did not use it. He gave in to the religious leaders because he did not want a riot and he did not want negative reports about his leadership reaching Rome.

On the other hand, Pilate's actions do not necessarily show weakness but rather his political awareness. Jerusalem was full of Jewish pilgrims for Passover and it would not have taken much for unrest to break out into violence. It was important for the stability of the country to compromise with the powerful religious leaders.

However, in spite of the politics of the situation, I think that Pilate was weak because he condemned a man he knew to be innocent. (7)

2 Jesus said to his disciples that they should be prepared to take up their cross and follow him. Taken at face value, this means that Christians should be prepared to die for others, just as Jesus did on the cross. Christian love is about sacrifice. Most of the time, sacrifice means giving up being selfish and putting others first. However, great acts of love can result in death – as it did for St Peter, Oscar Romero, Martin Luther King and many other martyrs.

However, giving up your life for your beliefs may not always be the right thing to do. Sometimes it would be far more loving to live and use one's gifts to help others. There is no virtue in putting yourself in a dangerous position, knowing this will result in death. This is, in fact, a very selfish thing to do and not the sign of a real martyr.

In conclusion, I don't think being willing to die for others is a sign of love. Knowing that one *might* die, on the other hand, is a sign of Christian love. (7)

3 Suffering is a fact of life but there is no reason why people should have to put up with it. Suffering is often caused by the selfishness and greed of others. It is a basic injustice that permits these people to enjoy their lives at the expense of others. The Golden Rule says that we should do to others as we would have them treat us. As no one chooses to suffer, then we have a duty to try to stop others suffering.

However, Jesus' teaching appeared to embrace suffering. He said he would suffer many things and his disciples would suffer. He even taught that love means being prepared to suffer for others. Suffering might be seen as a kind of test, just as Abraham was tested to see if he would sacrifice his only son Isaac. Many people put up with great suffering and we admire them because of their bravery.

I conclude that allowing people to suffer unnecessarily is not right. They should not be expected simply to put up with it. (7)

4 Some argue that capital punishment is always wrong because it is not Christian, it is cruel and it does not create a better society in which to live. Jesus specifically taught that the old law of 'an eye for an eye' should be replaced by the law of loving one's enemy. Finally, putting someone to death in cold blood reduces society to the same level as the criminal.

On the other hand, Jesus never specifically abolished the Old Testament laws on capital punishment and he said 'he who uses the sword shall die by the sword'. Capital punishment is the way in which society can express its disgust at things it finds to be morally totally unacceptable.

I think capital punishment should be used in the very rare cases where someone does something so bad that not to put them to death is allowing them and others to think that what they have done is not so bad. (7)

5   There were reasons for Jesus' death but they weren't good ones. Firstly, as Judas implied, Jesus could just have effectively taught about the Kingdom of God without deliberately dying as a martyr. Secondly, he could have explained to Pilate that he was not a political leader or king and therefore was no threat to Rome.

However, the point of Jesus' death was to challenge the Jewish idea of the messiah. As God's suffering servant, Jesus saw himself taking on the sins of the people and sacrificing himself for them. His death was also a way of showing how corrupt and evil humans could be. It reinforced his teaching about the Kingdom of God.

I think there were very good reasons for Jesus' death. His death was and is a challenge to the cruel way humans behave and it teaches us about the sacrifices we have to make to create civilised societies. (7)

6   Even if Joseph had placed Jesus' dead body in the tomb, there is no guarantee that during the night tomb robbers might not have come along and stolen his body. Perhaps they thought that as Jesus was 'King of the Jews' he might have been buried with his jewels. It is possible his followers stole the body because they wanted to invent a story about his Resurrection.

However, if this was the case, we would expect there to be other accounts that support it. It is likely that there would have been Roman soldiers keeping guard round the tomb in case of robbers. If Jesus' followers had stolen his body it still doesn't explain why hundreds of people claimed shortly afterwards to have experienced the risen Jesus.

It is very hard to know exactly what happened. I don't think the disciples made up experiencing the risen Jesus, but they may have been mistaken about the tomb being empty. (7)

7   In many ways it is true the women did show greater faith. Most of the disciples had run away at Gethsemane and then Peter had denied knowing Jesus. It was the women who had accompanied Jesus at his crucifixion and then came to anoint his body. Their loyalty contrasts considerably with that of the male disciples.

However, the women disciples had not had to experience first-hand the threats that Jesus had to go through. The male disciples had been there during all the various conflicts with the Jewish authorities during his ministry. They had even given up their jobs to follow him. It was understandable that faced by an armed guard at Gethsemane some should have fled.

In conclusion, the women did show considerable loyalty to Jesus but I don't think this is the same as faith. The male disciples may have wavered in their faith but I don't think they lost it. Therefore the women did not have greater faith than the male disciples. (7)

8   We are not told a great deal about Joseph of Arimathea so we can only really guess what his motives were. Perhaps he disliked the way the Sanhedrin had tried Jesus; it is possible that the trial was illegal because holding a criminal court at night was not permitted. Maybe he acted out of guilt and wanted at least to give Jesus a decent burial.

On the other hand, the Gospel says that Joseph was a leading member of the Sanhedrin and was also waiting for the Kingdom of God. This suggests that he must have known a lot more about Jesus' teaching and admired him. He was also brave as he went personally to Pilate and asked to take Jesus' body from the cross. He provided all the grave clothes to give Jesus a decent burial.

So, I think Joseph was the real hero of Jesus' burial. He was brave, generous and clearly admired Jesus. Without him, Jesus' body would have ended up in a common grave. (7)

9 Many argue that Jesus' burial is unimportant because it is his death and resurrection that are the key moments in the Gospel. The burial just links the two together and the story would work just as well without it. In fact, even if Jesus had not been put in Joseph's tomb, the Resurrection could still have taken place.

However, all the Gospels describe the burial in some detail because without it is there is nothing to show Jesus actually died and was buried. The event was witnessed by Joseph of Arimathea who was a senior member of the Sanhedrin and therefore trustworthy. Without the burial, it could be claimed that Jesus' body was stolen and the Resurrection was made up.

I think the burial is important. In the Christian creed it says that Jesus 'died and was buried' because without the story of the burial, the Resurrection would be far less dramatic. (7)

2.15 The Resurrection

Part a questions:

1 Resurrection means rising to new life from the dead. (2)

2 A miracle is an act of God that breaks the laws of physics. (2)

3 Blessed means being given true happiness by God. (2)

4 'Son of God' is the term used to describe Jesus' unique relationship with God. (2)

5 Simon Peter and the disciple who Jesus loved ran to the empty tomb. (2)

Part b questions:

1 Mary Magdalene arrived at the tomb early in the morning and when she saw the stone had been moved she ran and told Peter and the Beloved Disciple. The two disciples ran to the tomb and when Peter looked in he saw the linen cloths lying there neatly folded. Then the Beloved Disciple looked in and he saw and believed. (6)

2 Mary was outside the tomb and Jesus appeared and asked her why she was crying and who she was looking for. She thought he was the gardener and asked him if he had taken the body away and where he had put it. Jesus said, 'Mary' and then she recognised him and said, 'Rabboni!' Jesus warned her not to touch him because he had not yet ascended to the Father, to his God and her God. (6)

3 Mary was weeping outside the tomb when the angels asked why she was crying. She said that they had taken her Lord away and she didn't know where they had put him. Then she turned round and saw Jesus, but she didn't recognise him. He asked her the same question. She thought he was the gardener who had taken the body. Jesus said, 'Mary' and she realised who he was. Jesus told her not to touch him because he had not yet returned to his Father. (6)

4 The disciples were eating a meal behind locked doors when Jesus appeared and said, 'Peace be with you.' He showed them the marks of the crucifixion on his hands and feet. Then he said he was sending them off to preach. He breathed on them as a sign of receiving the Holy Spirit and gave them authority to forgive sins. (6)

5   Thomas had not been with the disciples and he said he would not believe Jesus had been raised unless he saw the marks of the crucifixion. A week later Jesus passed through locked doors and he told Thomas to put his finger in the marks on his hands and his side. Thomas said, 'My Lord and my God'. Jesus said that those who believed without seeing were also blessed. (6)

Part c questions:

1   By appearing to Mary first Jesus shows that the old Jewish rules that separated men and women no longer apply. It is also significant because no female witness would be taken seriously in the first century and yet it is Mary who first experiences the Resurrection. Many women had been Jesus' faithful followers and remained with him even when the male disciples left. Mary's faith therefore contrasts with the lack of faith of the men. (6)

2   Thomas had not been at the discovery of the empty tomb nor had he been in the room when the disciples first encountered the risen Jesus. He said he would not believe unless he had seen and touched Jesus' wounds. Then Jesus appeared and Thomas believed. These words stress that belief in the Resurrection comes through a deep understanding of who Jesus is and what the Resurrection means and does not require physical proof. (6)

3   For some Christians, the empty tomb means that Jesus' body had actually been resurrected. The linen cloths lying neatly in the tomb suggest that the body wasn't snatched by tomb robbers but had been deliberately transformed by God. Other Christians see the empty tomb as a symbol of new life. It is a sign that death is not the end and that the Resurrection is the start of a new kind of life. (6)

4   Jesus said this to Thomas because Thomas represents all those who find Jesus' death and Resurrection very difficult to understand. Thomas wanted physical proof of Jesus' Resurrection but he hadn't really understood that the Resurrection is not just about believing in Jesus' transformed body but rather his message about transforming one's life and the world. Jesus' teaching was about the Good News and the Kingdom of God and that is what Thomas needed to think about. (6)

5   Jesus breathed on the disciples because this is how John's Gospel describes Pentecost. It is a sign that the disciples would continue Jesus' work guided by the Holy Spirit in their hearts. God had breathed into Adam when he created him and given him life, so when Jesus breathes on the disciples he is inspiring them to live new lives and preach the Good News. (6)

Part d questions:

1   Some people might say that Thomas is the most important character in the Resurrection story because he is the one who demanded concrete proof. This is an attitude perfectly in tune with today's thinking and one that gives hope to modern Christians who experience doubt. He was also important because he touched the wounds of crucifixion, thus confirming that Jesus' resurrection was real.

On the other hand, it could be argued that Mary played a bigger role than Thomas because she carried the message of Jesus' resurrection to the other disciples. It is also significant that while Thomas needed physical evidence of Jesus' resurrection, Jesus commended those who would believe without having seen. Those are the people who would spread the gospel in the future.

I conclude, therefore, that it is not Thomas who is the most important person in the story, but those like Mary and future believers who showed greater faith. (7)

2 Some argue that the Resurrection must be the most important thing in Christianity because no one else has ever died and reappeared. This unique aspect of Christianity shows how Jesus' death was not the end and promises life beyond death. It also turns his death into a victory over sin and the evil in the world that had led to his crucifixion.

However, on the other hand, Resurrection is only one aspect of Jesus' life. There is also his teaching, his treatment of the marginalised and his challenge to religious and political authorities. Christians such as Trevor Huddleston have made these aspects of their beliefs central to countering racism and other social injustices.

In conclusion, I don't think the statement is right. Although the Resurrection might be important, for most of the time what Christianity stands for is how we treat others. (7)

3 Many scientists argue that miracles cannot happen because there are much better explanations of unusual events than saying they are miracles. For a miracle to occur it would have to break the laws of physics. This is a contradiction. For example, if a one-legged person grew another leg overnight we would have to conclude that there was a law of nature that we had overlooked, however unlikely this might appear. There would be no need to call it a miracle.

However, there are other scientists who argue that it is reasonable to allow for miracles. Science can only make predictions about what will happen, so a very, very unlikely event could happen even though there appeared to be no way we could calculate it. This is why the Resurrection is possible as a miracle.

In conclusion, I don't think science rejects the possibility of miracles. However, I also don't think it accepts that the Resurrection is 'entirely' possible. (7)

4 Many argue that any so-called evidence for life after death can be dismissed scientifically. For example, some people claim to have had near-death experiences in which their soul leaves their body and makes a journey to heaven. However, this can be explained as hallucinations caused by lack of oxygen to the brain. It also makes more sense to say this is our only life and we should make the most of it now.

On the other hand, Christianity is not the only religion to argue for life after death. Islam also states that life after death is the means by which God judges and rewards those who have lived good lives and punishes those who have not. This makes much more sense of our lives, as there is little point being good if bad people appear to live happier lives.

In conclusion, I don't think there is life after death. Most people who argue for life after death do so because they don't like the idea of dying and the idea of life after death makes them feel better. (7)

5 There are many philosophers who agree with this statement. Doubting is not a negative but a good way to test ideas and beliefs. For example, it would be entirely reasonable for me to doubt the existence of fairies unless someone could give me very good reasons and evidence to prove that they actually existed. Furthermore, there are some beliefs that could be very dangerous to hold, for example in the times of American slavery, the belief that slaves are not fully human.

However, not all beliefs can be proved completely. I might believe in the power of love but it is not something for which I can provide scientific evidence. I might also believe that God exists because millions of others have found that it has helped to make sense of their lives. Doubting these ideas does not help make these beliefs clearer; in fact it does the opposite and confuses them.

In conclusion, I agree with the statement. Doubting is an important process in believing. I don't think it destroys beliefs, but makes them stronger. (7)

3 Contemporary issues

3.1 Science and religion

1   Richard Dawkins believes that science is incompatible with religion. Science tests its answers but religion does not. This is why Darwin's theory of evolution is more likely to be right than Genesis. Dawkins holds that followers of religion today are deluded because there is no God. He states that religion is the cause of much of the evil in the world. (6)

2   Creationism is the belief that the Bible has more authority than science when it comes to understanding the origins of the universe. For example, creationists believe that God created everything exactly as it says in Genesis 1 and that science is wrong. They say that human beings were specially created and are not the random product of evolution. (6)

3   Intelligent design is a variation of the creationist argument. Creationists believe that Genesis offers a better account of the creation of the world than science. Intelligent design supports this view by arguing that some things, such as the human eye, are so carefully constructed that they must have been designed by an intelligent being – God. (6)

4   Christians think science and religion are compatible because they look at things in different ways. Religion tells us why things happen and science tells us how. Another reason is that the laws of science that govern the universe are sustained by God so they work together. Thirdly, evolution does not contradict Genesis because God created the process by which life evolved. (6)

5   Stephen Hawking believes that the universe began 15 billion years ago with what is known as the Big Bang. This event started everything and led eventually to human existence. The universe spontaneously created itself according to the laws of science. He says we can explain how this happened without involving God. (6)

3.2 Stewardship and the environment

1   A Rocha is a conservation organisation. It runs environmental educational programmes to train people to restore and protect natural animal habitats. It has projects all over the world, such as ecotourism in Kenya and restoring salmon streams in Canada. Its 'Living Lightly' project helps Christians to be good stewards of the world in their everyday lives. (6)

2   Christians teach that God appointed humans to be His stewards by keeping the earth in good order. God made a covenant with humans that as they care for the world, He will love and bless them. One day God will make the world perfect again but before that humans have to repair the damage they have caused. (6)

3   One example of environmental crisis is global warming, which is caused by damage to the ozone layer. This is causing the planet to get too hot. Another example is pollution caused by waste products. A third example is the destruction of the Amazon rainforests and the effects of this on wildlife and the production of oxygen. (6)

4   People should protect the environment so that future generations can enjoy it and make use of its resources. They should also protect it because it is a justice issue. Those who suffer as a result of environmental crises are the poorest and least able to help themselves. People also have a duty to protect animal habitats and food supplies. (6)

5   We can think 'green' by recycling what would otherwise go to landfill. We can reduce fuel consumption by using alternative forms of power. Governments can work together as they did at the Copenhagen Summit of 2009 to agree measures to reduce climate change. We can educate people to improve their understanding of the world and the effects of their actions. (6)

3.3 Stewardship and animals

1   One reason why humans have treated animals differently is that humans do not think that animals are conscious or have souls. If that is the case, they don't feel pain as humans do and can be treated differently. The second reason is that animals do not make moral decisions and therefore are not entitled to the same rights as humans. (6)

2   One reason for vegetarianism is that God gave human beings special responsibility to look after the planet and to rule over the animals. In Eden, animals and humans lived in harmony, so this means God always intended humans to be vegetarians. The second reason is that if we don't have to eat meat we should not do so – we can still live healthily. (6)

3   Humans have used animals for research to test new potentially life-saving drugs. The drugs have to be tested for harmful side effects as well as to see whether they really work. Because the drugs are at the experimental stage, it is not safe to test them on humans. Many people's lives have been saved because of this research. (6)

4   Many people think that as animals are not conscious in the same way as humans, they don't have the same rights as humans. This means that providing humans don't cause them deliberate harm, it is acceptable to use animals for human entertainment (as pets or in circuses) if they give us pleasure. (6)

5   Many Christians argue for vegetarianism because the Bible says humans have a duty to be good stewards of the animals in the world. This means that as humans don't need to eat meat to survive then killing animals for food would be causing them unnecessary pain. In Genesis 2 humans live in harmony with animals without killing and eating them. (6)

3.4 Human rights

1   Human rights are a way of protecting human beings against exploitation by others or by the state. They are a way of respecting human dignity. All humans are entitled to life, freedom and happiness. Basic human rights should not be taken away. (6)

2   Children's rights are also human rights. However, children are entitled to certain rights because they are more vulnerable than adults and while they are growing up they have particular needs. These rights might include survival, family, education and protection against exploitation. (6)

3   King was a black Christian minister. When he was growing up there was segregation in the southern states of the USA – black people had to attend different schools, churches and universities from white people. King campaigned, using non-violent protest (such as his march on Washington), to give black people the same rights as white people. (6)

4 Christian teaching supports human rights because Jesus frequently sided with the poor, the oppressed and the exploited. In his parable of the Sheep and the Goats he said, 'Whatever you did for one of the least of these brothers of mine, you did for me.' He told his disciples off for not treating children with respect. (6)

5 UNICEF is the United Nations Children's Fund. It was created in 1946 to provide healthcare for children after the Second World War. It is the only organisation mentioned in the UN Convention on the Rights of the Child. Its motto is 'Denying a child rights is wrong. Put it right.' (6)

3.5 Laws and rules

1 The Rule of St Benedict is a set of rules that monks have to follow. It tells monks when to pray, how they should speak to each other and what they should wear. This is so the monks can live in a Christian community and be faithful to the teachings of Christ. (6)

2 Moral relativism is the belief that there are no absolute rights and wrongs. This is based on the fact that we all have different views and different values. Moral relativists believe that our values change over time. Moral relativists don't think the Ten Commandments are absolute rules because, for example, it might sometimes be necessary to steal or kill. (6)

3 Punishment is used to deter people so that they do not reoffend. It is there as retribution to make offenders suffer for their crimes and shows them that society will not put up with their law-breaking. Punishment is also to help people understand that what they did was wrong and reform them into law-abiding citizens. (6)

4 The Prison Reform Trust argues that prisons should only be used as a last resort when all other methods of punishment have been considered. It argues that Britain has too many prisoners and that prison frequently does not make prisoners better people. Prison should prepare inmates with skills to go back into society. (6)

5 Capital punishment is a unique deterrent. It makes sure that the murderer does not kill again. It allows the families of victims to feel that justice has been done and may help them to come to terms with their loss. Some Christians justify it by quoting Jesus' saying that those who use the sword will die by the sword. (6)

3.6 Leadership and wisdom

1 Conscience, for Christians and other religious people, is the way in which God communicates what is right and wrong. Conscience might be living by God's Commandments given in the Bible. For atheists, conscience is a strong feeling of what ought to be done. This might mean following the Golden Rule or standing up for human rights. (6)

2 In the Sermon on the Mount, Jesus taught the disciples that although they had been told to hate their enemies, they should instead love them. He taught that just as God shows mercy to humans, so we should show mercy to our enemies. (6)

3 Bonhoeffer showed extreme Christian courage and leadership. He was a Christian pastor in Germany and could have had a career teaching at a university in the USA. Instead he chose to go back to Nazi Germany and to be involved in the plot to assassinate Hitler. He helped the Confessing Church to train up new pastors, even though the Nazis had forbidden this. (6)

4 A good leader might be like King Solomon, who acted wisely. Good leaders must put the needs of others above their own. They must practise what they preach; as Jesus said, 'no good tree bears bad fruit'. They must set themselves high moral standards and have humility by being a servant to others. (6)

5 Harold Shipman abused his power as a doctor. He murdered many of his elderly patients while pretending to help them. Many thought he was a kind doctor but in fact he just enjoyed using his power. Soldiers in war sometimes misuse their power by torturing prisoners, in some cases purely for entertainment. This is an abuse of the prisoners' human rights. (6)

3.7 Social justice

1 Social justice is treating everyone equally according to their needs. It is based on the idea that humans were created in the image of God and no one is more or less valuable than anyone else. There is a need for a law to uphold social justice because humans sometimes exploit each other. Social justice means providing for all those in need. (6)

2 Fair Trade is an international movement that ensures producers in poor countries get a fair deal and can make a profit. They are given proper long-term contracts and often receive training in the skills they need to develop their business. The workers are not exploited and have decent working conditions and a fair wage. (6)

3 Jackie Pullinger works with drug addicts in Hong Kong. She talks to them on the streets and tells them about Jesus. She has set up houses like St Stephen's for addicts where they can come off drugs through prayer and receive medical help and teaching. She continues to work with addicts even when they abuse her care. (6)

4 In Genesis 1 God commanded humans to subdue the earth and rule over the animals as His stewards. To be a steward means to act on behalf of another, so humans have the responsibility of carrying on God's work on earth. That means caring for the environment. Social justice means caring for the poor and the weak and making sure they are provided for. (6)

5 Romero was Archbishop of San Salvador at a time of political unrest. Rich landowners exploited the poor and murdered anyone who opposed them. Romero defended the workers and spoke up for them. He campaigned for justice in his sermons and refused to attend any government functions until workers were treated fairly. He was murdered for his outspokenness. (6)

3.8 Treatment of the poor

1 Jesus challenged the view that wealth was a sign of God's blessing. In the story of the rich young man, Jesus said that if he wanted to be good, he should give all his money to the poor. Some people say this is what all Christians should do, while others say it is a reminder of the responsibilities the rich have towards the poor. (6)

2 Mother Teresa began her work by taking medicines and food to the people in the slums of Calcutta. She founded the 'Missionaries of Charity' and set up schools for the poor and hospices for people with leprosy, such as Nirmal Hriday. She provided a home for the dying so that they did not have to die in the street. (6)

3   Charity is central to Christianity because it is central to Jesus' teaching. He said he came to serve, not to be served, and to give his life as a sacrifice for others. Because God gave generously out of His love, Christians also should act generously. They should support justice and provide for the needs of the poor.   (6)

4   The rich young man wanted to know how he could inherit eternal life. Jesus reminded him of the social Commandments and the young man said he had kept them all his life. Jesus then said he lacked one thing. He was to sell everything he had and give to the poor. The man went away sad because he was very rich.   (6)

5   Trevor Huddleston was a priest who campaigned against apartheid in South Africa. He worked in a squatter township called Sophiatown. He supported the African National Congress and fought for equal rights for black South Africans. He spoke out against the government's unjust policies towards them and worked hard to bring apartheid to an end.   (6)

3.9 Prejudice and discrimination

1   Prejudice is pre-judging someone with little or no evidence. Discrimination is acting negatively towards some people but not others. If people are treated differently because of prejudiced opinions, it leads to injustice. For example, someone might be refused a job because he or she belongs to a group of people the employer is prejudiced against. This injustice is a violation of human rights.   (6)

2   A multi-racial society is one that tolerates having many different racial types of people living together – hopefully in harmony. A plural society is one that allows for many different beliefs to exist side by side. This means different religions can worship and people can have different political and moral beliefs.   (6)

3   Meg Guillebaud's work promoted reconciliation between Hutu and Tutsi tribes in Rwanda after the genocide. She trained church leaders from both tribes so they could bring about reconciliation in their village congregations. She also started sewing groups to provide women with income and encouraged people to talk about their experiences and begin the process of forgiving those who had wronged them.   (6)

4   Prejudice is to hold a generalised and often irrational view about a person or group of people. This might be based on stereotypes learned through the internet or the views of one's family and friends. It is negative. Discrimination means to act against a person or group based on one's prejudice. An example is not giving a job to someone who is qualified for it, just because that person is black.   (6)

5   There are laws in the UK to stop people discriminating against others because of their sex, race and disability. These laws state that all people should have the right to equal pay, job opportunities and benefits regardless of their race, sex or disability.   (6)

3.10 Attitudes to death

1   Many Christians argue that euthanasia is wrong because God gave humans life as a gift; it is therefore not ours to get rid of. It is against the Ten Commandments to take an innocent life. Finally, it is a Christian duty to help the sick and dying, as Jesus helped the sick; killing a sick person is not good medicine.   (6)

2 Humanists who are nihilists believe that humans do not have souls so when a person dies that is the end. They believe there is no afterlife so there is nothing to fear about death as once you are dead you completely cease to exist. Humanists believe that a person lives on only in the memories of others. (6)

3 The Christian 'sanctity of life' argument says that all human life is special and must be protected. This is because God created humans in His own image. This means that if humans have a spark of God in them, life must be protected as it is holy. Jesus taught that we must love one another and respect everyone, even our enemies. (6)

4 Cicely Saunders started the hospice movement in St Thomas's Hospital in London after she had visited a patient who was suffering from cancer. He said how much her visits meant to him. He left her £500 in his will and she used the money to help others who were dying by opening St Christopher's hospice in 1967. (6)

5 The 'quality of life' argument does not accept that human lives are God-given. That means that a life is only worth living when a person is happy, free from pain and can do what they want. This means that choosing euthanasia, for example, depends on the individual's decision about whether their life is worthwhile. (6)

3.11 War and peace

1 For a war to be 'just' it must be controlled by a government and not an independent group. The cause itself must be something like self-defence or the protection of innocent people. It must also only be a last resort after all other avenues have been tried, and the goal must be to restore peace and justice. (6)

2 Pacifists believe that all human life is sacred or special, and therefore that it is always wrong to kill a person deliberately. Quakers, for example, believe this. Weak pacifists argue that this is generally true but that in some extreme circumstances killing would be more moral when it protects innocent people from greater harm. Some weak pacifists support the 'just war' argument. (6)

3 Quakers are absolute pacifists because they believe that all killing is always wrong. Human lives all have a spark of God and therefore deliberately to kill anyone is blasphemy and violates what we value in ourselves. They argue that humans have the power to create just and fair societies without ever resorting to violence. (6)

4 Some Christians argue that Jesus' teaching in the Sermon on the Mount only set up an ideal of pacifism; he never condemned anyone for being a soldier. He also taught that Christians have a duty to obey the state and therefore if the state commands someone to fight then they must do so. Many Christians support the 'just war' argument. (6)

5 One reason for going to war might be that a country has been attacked by another and is therefore defending itself. Another reason could be that a country is doing evil things (such as massacres) and the war is waged in order to overcome evil and promote good. Finally, war might be the last resort when all other means have broken down. (6)

4 Christianity

4.1 Jesus

1 Jesus was called Messiah or Christ, which means the anointed one. Jesus was the Messiah who would save human beings from their sin. He was called the Son of Man, which identifies him with human suffering. The Son of Man would also act as judge. The title Son of God shows his special relationship with God. (6)

2 Jesus was baptised by John in the River Jordan, after which he fasted in the desert. The devil tempted him there but Jesus resisted him. During his ministry, Jesus performed miracles such as healing the paralysed man. He was betrayed by Judas, one of his disciples, and executed by Pontius Pilate. He rose from the dead three days later. (6)

3 Christians believe that Jesus is the second person of the Trinity and God incarnate. He died to save human beings from their sin. He rose from the dead as a sign of his victory over sin and death and ascended to heaven. Anyone who believes in him will have eternal life. Jesus will return to judge the world. (6)

4 Christians believe that God created the world and everything in it and wants a relationship with human beings. He is a God of love and is called 'Father'. They believe that Jesus is the Son of God. He was born into the world to save people from sin by dying on the cross. He rose from the dead and ascended to heaven. (6)

5 Jesus taught that God loved the world so much that He gave His son to die so that people could be forgiven. He taught that people should love each other as they love God. He taught that people should prepare for the Kingdom of God. He said that anyone who believed in him would not die but would have eternal life. (6)

4.2 The Bible

1 The Bible is important to Christians because they believe it is the inspired word of God and tells them about Him. It is a record of Jesus' life and teaching and also the teaching of the first apostles. It shows Christians how to live their lives. It helps them in times of difficulty and God speaks to them through it. (6)

2 The Bible is not always easy to understand. For example, there are some very violent stories in the Old Testament and many people think they clash with what Jesus taught about love. Today, people find it hard to believe that the miracles really happened. It is difficult to know whether some stories in the Bible are literal or symbolic. (6)

3 The Old Testament is a set of books containing the Jewish Scriptures. The Law is contained in the first five books. It is also a history book recording events in the lives of the Jews. It contains books of poetry such as the Psalms and the writings of the prophets. Jews and Christians believe it is the word of God. (6)

4   The New Testament is a collection of books and letters. The Gospels contain stories of the life, death and resurrection of Jesus. The book of Acts is a record of the beginnings of the Christian church. There are many letters written by Christian leaders, such as St Paul, to leaders in Christian communities across Asia. (6)

5   The Gospels were written by four men – Matthew, Mark, Luke and John. They are about Jesus' life, death and resurrection. They contain his teaching about the Kingdom of God, his Sermon on the Mount and stories of his miracles. The word 'gospel' means good news. (6)

4.3 Beliefs

1   Christians believe that God is love and that He exists in three persons: God the Father, who made the world; God the Son, who saved human beings; and God the Holy Spirit, who inspires them. They believe in the forgiveness of sins and the resurrection of the dead to new life in heaven. (6)

2   Christians mean one God who exists in three persons. God the Father, who made the world, is the first person. The second person is God the Son. The son became human (as Jesus) and redeemed the world. The third person of the Trinity is the Holy Spirit, who is the power of God at work in the world. (6)

3   As he did after Pentecost, the Holy Spirit gives courage and strength to Christians as they try to do the will of God. He comforts and encourages people in times of trouble and sadness. He helps people with their prayers and inspires them to speak about their faith by revealing God's truth to them. (6)

4   The incarnation is the belief that God came to earth in human form in the person of Jesus. Jesus was completely human and yet wholly God at the same time. Incarnation literally means 'in the flesh', so God experienced what it was like to be human so that He could save people from their sins. (6)

5   Christians believe that they will go to heaven when they die. God will judge them according to their lives on earth. They will see family and friends again, although heaven is a spiritual place beyond time and space. They will be in God's presence and will worship Him for ever. (6)

4.4 Baptism

1   The parents and godparents promise to bring the baby up in a Christian way. The priest asks the parents to name the child and he then pours water from the font over the baby's head. He makes the sign of the cross on his or her forehead and the baby becomes a part of the Church family. (6)

2   At a typical believer's baptism, the person being baptised repents of his sins and gives a testimony saying why he is a Christian. He enters the water, which can be a river or pool, and the pastor holds his head and his hand. The pastor plunges the person under the water and brings him up again. (6)

3   Water in baptism is a symbol of washing away sins. Water is also a symbol of the end of one life and the beginning of a new one. Light is a symbol of Jesus' presence. He described himself as the 'light of the world'. Light also symbolises how a person passes from darkness to light. (6)

4   At an Orthodox baptism, the baby is immersed in the water three times. The priest raises the Gospel over the baby and prays for him to be free from evil. He makes the sign of the cross

using blessed oil. This is called the Chrismation. Three pieces of hair are taken to show his life is dedicated to God. A lighted candle is given. (6)

5 Baptism is when a person becomes a Christian because the water symbolises washing away sin and starting a new life in Christ. At adult baptism a person confesses their sins and promises to follow Christ's teachings. At an infant baptism parents and godparents make promises to bring up the child according to Christian teaching. (6)

4.5 Prayer

1 Christians pray in different ways and they can kneel, sit or stand while they do it. Most people close their eyes so that they can focus on God. Some will use icons or pray to a particular saint. Christians can pray in private or worship with others in church. Many pray using the Lord's Prayer. (6)

2 Christians pray to God as an act of worship. It draws them closer to God. They praise Him for who He is and what He has done. They pray for forgiveness and because they want to ask for guidance or help in a particular situation. They might pray for someone else. (6)

3 The Lord's Prayer is what Jesus taught his disciples as a model for how they should pray. It begins with adoration of God. This is followed by the request for daily needs. Then they ask God to forgive their sins. Finally there is a plea for God's help in times of temptation. It ends with praise of God's power and glory. (6)

4 Christians often use icons or pictures to help them pray. Some look at a cross or hold one in their hands. Others use a rosary and many people light candles. Some Christians have statues of Mary or one of the saints in their homes. They may kneel as a sign of humility or cross themselves. (6)

5 Prayers of thanks are when you remember God's goodness and everything He has done for you. Prayers of intercession are when you ask God to do something for someone or for yourself, for example praying that a sick relative gets better. Prayers of guidance are when you ask for help in a specific situation when you don't know what to do. (6)

4.6 Places of worship

1 The main feature in a typical Orthodox church is the iconostasis, which stands across the east end of the church. It is covered with icons and is often very ornate. There are icons in other parts of the church as well. There are always candles burning. The font is usually just inside the west door. There are no pews. (6)

2 The altar with cross or crucifix on it is in the east end of a typical Anglican church. The nave is filled with pews for seating. There is a pulpit for preaching and a lectern that holds the Bible. The font is usually just inside the west door. Most churches have an organ and many have stained glass windows. (6)

3 The pulpit is where the priest stands to give his sermon. The height above the congregation gives him authority and enables everyone to see him. The lectern, often carved in the shape of an eagle, holds the Bible. It is read in most services. The altar is where the people come to receive Holy Communion. (6)

4 Baptist churches are simply decorated. There is a raised pulpit in the middle at the front and the Lord's Table is placed in front of it. There will be a small pool under the floor for baptisms. Chairs or pews are placed in rows for people to sit on and there is an organ or piano. (6)

5. Roman Catholic churches have the altar at the east end with a crucifix on it. The pulpit is at the front and to the side. There will be a statue of the Virgin Mary. There is a lectern at the front and a font by the west door. Walls may have pictures on them showing the Stations of the Cross. (6)

4.7 Holy Communion

1. At a service of Holy Communion Christians remember the Last Supper when Jesus gave his disciples bread and wine. Hymns are sung and prayers are said. People repent of their sins. There are readings from the Bible and the priest gives a sermon. The people come up to the altar to receive the bread and the wine. (6)

2. Christians celebrate Holy Communion to remember the new covenant Jesus made with human beings on the night before he died. When they eat the bread and drink the wine they remember that Jesus' body was broken on the cross and his blood was shed to save them from their sin. Celebrating Holy Communion is a way of sharing their faith with all Christians. (6)

3. The bread is a symbol of Jesus' body and the wine is a symbol of his blood. By eating the bread and drinking the wine Christians remember that Jesus shed his blood and died for them. Water is added to the wine. This represents the blood and the water that came out of Jesus' side when he was on the cross. (6)

4. Church services often include the singing of hymns and songs. There is usually a reading from the Bible and a sermon either explaining the reading or on a topical issue. Prayers are said such as the Lord's Prayer and prayers of confession and intercession. A creed or statement of belief may be said and there may be Holy Communion as part of the service. (6)

5. In Anglican churches people go up to the altar to receive the bread and wine. In Methodist churches, communion is often brought to them and passed along the rows in little racks of glasses containing non-alcoholic wine. In Orthodox churches the priest brings the bread soaked in wine on a spoon to each member of the congregation. (6)

4.8 Marriage

1. In a typical marriage service, the minister explains the purpose of marriage and then the bride and groom make vows to each other. They promise to love each other and be faithful, to honour and protect each other as long as they live. They exchange rings and the minister pronounces them husband and wife. (6)

2. The bride and groom promise to love, honour and protect each other and be faithful to each other for the rest of their lives. To love means to cherish and comfort one another in good times and bad. To honour and protect means to respect and look out for each other. Being faithful means not committing adultery. (6)

3. All Christians agree that marriage is a sacred vow and divorce is a serious matter. Traditional Protestant Christian teaching says that the only valid reason for divorce is unfaithfulness. Roman Catholics forbid divorce. Many Protestant churches are sympathetic to the idea that relationships can break down and that divorce can prevent unhappiness and help people to move on. (6)

4. The bride and groom promise to love each other and to be faithful to each other for the rest of their lives. They promise to stay together for better or worse, for richer or poorer, in sickness and in health. They promise to love, comfort, honour and protect each other. (6)

5 The first purpose of Christian marriage is to provide a safe environment in which to raise children. The second purpose is to protect each other from sin. Each promises to be faithful to the other. The third purpose is for the couple to grow in love and companionship together. Each provides comfort and support for the other. (6)

4.9 Holy Week and Easter

1 Holy Week starts with Palm Sunday when Christians remember Jesus' triumphal entry into Jerusalem riding on a donkey. People threw palm branches down and shouted 'Hosanna!' On Maundy Thursday Christians remember the Last Supper and how Jesus washed the disciples' feet. They remember the crucifixion of Jesus on Good Friday and his lying buried in the tomb on Holy Saturday. (6)

2 On Easter Sunday, Christians decorate the church with flowers and sing hymns celebrating the resurrection of Jesus from the dead. Most churches hold services of Holy Communion. There are readings from the Bible and prayers of thanksgiving. People give each other chocolate eggs or rabbits as a reminder of new life in Christ. (6)

3 On Good Friday Christians remember the death of Jesus. They think about his arrest and trial before the High Priest and then Pilate. During a three-hour vigil, they remember his crucifixion and burial. Easter Day is a time of rejoicing as they remember Jesus' Resurrection and how he appeared to Mary and his disciples. (6)

4 The purpose of Holy Week for Christians is to prepare their hearts and minds for Easter. On Palm Sunday this means thinking about Jesus' Kingship. On Maundy Thursday it means thinking about how being a Christian involves service to others. On Good Friday and Holy Saturday, Christians realise the extent of what Jesus did for them on the cross. (6)

5 During Lent, Christians prepare for Easter. Lent begins on Ash Wednesday when ashes smeared on the forehead remind people of their sins. Many Christians fast during this time or give something up to remember Jesus fasting and being tempted in the wilderness. Christians may also take something up during Lent in preparation for Holy Week and Easter, such as attending a Lent course or reading the bible and praying more. (6)

4.10 Festivals

1 At Harvest Festival, people decorate the church with fruit and vegetables to celebrate God's provision for them. A harvest loaf decorated with wheat sheaves is usually placed by the altar. This is all distributed among the elderly and needy of the parish afterwards. Most churches will host a Harvest supper for the parish. Hymns of praise are sung. (6)

2 At Pentecost (or Whitsun), Christians remember the birth of the Church. It is the time when the Holy Spirit was first given to the apostles as tongues of fire, enabling them to preach the gospel by giving them the ability to speak in different languages. Pentecost is therefore traditionally a time when new believers are baptised. (6)

3 At Christmas, Christians remember the incarnation. God, in Jesus, became a human being and was born as a baby in Bethlehem. People remember that God's purpose in sending Jesus was to save the world from sin. They remember how the baby Jesus was visited by the wise men and shepherds. Prayers are said for the poor and the sick. (6)

4   At Pentecost, Christians remember the coming of the Holy Spirit. It marks the beginning of the Christian Church. Today, Christians attend services and some take part in walks of witness, remembering the witness of the Apostles. It is also known as Whitsun because traditionally new believers are baptised and women wear white dresses. (6)

5   Advent includes four Sundays and is a time of preparation, getting ready to celebrate Christmas and remembering Jesus' first coming as a baby. It is also a time recalling Jesus' promise that he would return again. During Advent, Christians may have Advent calendars, candles or wreaths that count down to Christmas. There are also special services such as the Christingle and Advent Carol Services. (6)

4.11 Pilgrimage

1   Christians go to Canterbury because it is the seat of the senior bishop in the Church of England. St Thomas à Becket, the twelfth-century archbishop, was murdered there and some claim they have been healed at his tomb. Christians go to Walsingham to find peace and healing at the holy spring where Lady Richeldis had a vision of Mary in 1061. (6)

2   Christians go to Israel because they feel that they can get closer to Jesus if they can see the places where he lived and taught. For example, visiting Galilee and Jerusalem might help them to understand his teaching better. In the same way, when they see where he died they can appreciate more fully what his death meant. (6)

3   Rome is an important place for pilgrims to visit because it is where the Pope lives and he is the head of the Roman Catholic Church. The Pope is the successor of St Peter, who is buried under St Peter's Church in the Vatican. Pilgrims also visit the catacombs where early Christians worshipped God and were buried. (6)

4   On pilgrimage to Israel, Christians see the Church of the Nativity at Bethlehem and go to Galilee where Jesus did much of his teaching, such as the Sermon on the Mount. They follow the route he took in Jerusalem to his crucifixion and visit the place where he was buried. (6)

5   People go on pilgrimage to Lourdes in the hope of being healed. They visit the church that was built over a cave, where in 1858 a French girl saw a vision of St Mary. A spring of water appeared and it is said to have healing powers. People receive counselling for illness and prayers are said. (6)

5 Judaism

5.1 Abraham and Moses

1   Moses escaped death as a baby and was brought up by an Egyptian princess. He killed an Egyptian taskmaster, who was beating an Israelite slave, and had to leave. He went to Midian, where God told him to rescue the Israelites from Pharaoh. He led them out of Egypt and through the desert. God gave him the Law at Sinai. (6)

2   Abraham was a nomad who lived in Ur and travelled in Mesopotamia. One day he felt that God had called him to go to Canaan. God made a covenant with him that he would be the father of a great nation and have land and many descendants. On another occasion, God tested Abraham's faith by telling him to sacrifice his only son Isaac. (6)

3   When Pharaoh refused to let the Israelites go, God sent ten plagues. The last one was the death of every firstborn creature. The Israelites put the blood of a lamb on their doors and the angel of death passed over their houses. Then Pharaoh said they could go and Moses led them through the Red Sea to freedom. (6)

4   The Exodus was when God called Moses to escape from Egypt to go to Canaan. It began when God sent ten plagues to persuade Pharaoh to let the children of Israel go. After the tenth plague (death of the firstborn) they escaped by night and passed through the Red Sea. In the wilderness God gave Moses the Torah. (6)

5   God sent ten plagues when Pharaoh would not let the Israelites go. The tenth was the death of every firstborn. God told the Israelites to kill a lamb and smear blood on their door posts. This would be a sign to the angel of death who would pass over them. They then escaped from Egypt through the Red Sea. (6)

5.2 Holy books

1   Orthodox Jews believe that the Torah was given to Moses. It is the first five books of the Tenach and contains 613 commandments or mitzvoth. The Ten Commandments are the central mitzvoth. The Talmud contains stories and teachings of the rabbis on how to keep the Torah. It contains the Oral Torah, which God also gave to Moses. (6)

2   The Tenach contains three sets of writings. First is the Torah or Law, which are the first five books. Then there are the Nevi'im or Prophets. The books of the prophets include Jeremiah, Isaiah and Ezekiel. Finally there are the Ketuvim or Writings. Examples of the Writings include the Psalms and Proverbs. (6)

3   The Written Torah is the Law that was given directly by God. It is the first five books of the Jewish Bible. It is the covenant that God made with Moses and contains 613 commandments. The Oral Torah was given to Moses at the same time as the Written Torah, which the rabbis later interpreted. (6)

4 The Torah means 'teaching' and contains written laws. There are 613 commandments or mitzvoth, which cover every aspect of life. It describes the covenant God made with Moses. The Ten Commandments are the heart of the covenant. The first five books of the Torah include Exodus and Deuteronomy. (6)

5 The Torah scroll, or Sefer Torah, is kept in the ark. During the service it is laid out on the bimah and opened at the appropriate place. A special pointer is used to guide the reader. The words are in Hebrew. At the end of the worship, the scroll is held up and a prayer is said before placing the scroll back in the ark. (6)

5.3 Beliefs

1 Jews believe that God is one and that He created the world. He knows everything. He gave humans the law so they can worship Him and live life to the full. Jews are waiting for the Messiah, whom they believe is God's messenger of peace. When he comes everyone will obey the Commandments. (6)

2 The world to come or Olam Ha'Ba is a time when God will bring this world to an end and establish an eternal state of peace, which will last for ever. No one is quite sure what it will be like. Some Jews argue that it will be an afterlife in heaven. Others say it will just be this world, transformed and perfect. (6)

3 The most important thing that Jews believe about God is that He is one and there are no other gods. They believe He created the world and knows and sees everything that happens. God gave the Jews the Torah so that they might worship Him with all their hearts and minds and soul as the Shema states. (6)

4 Many Jews believe that the Messiah will be God's specially chosen messenger of peace. When he arrives everyone will obey the Commandments and live in peace and harmony with each other. Many Jews are still expecting him to arrive. Some think he is not a person but a state of peace in the world. (6)

5 The Shema is very important for Jews. It means 'hear' because it starts by telling Israel to hear that God is one and He alone will be worshipped with all one's heart and mind and soul. It is said daily. A parchment containing the Shema is placed in a mezuzah case and tefillin. A Jew should recite it just before death. (6)

5.4 Synagogue

1 The tefillin are special prayer boxes. Jewish men wear two. One is strapped to their arm next to the blood vessel leading to the heart. The other is attached to their forehead, which is next to the brain. They contain the Shema. Wearing them reminds the person, in heart and mind, that the Lord is one God. (6)

2 In accordance with the Torah, the tallit is worn by men and boys over the age of 13 for worship in the synagogue. They drape the shawl around their shoulders. It has tassels at each corner. Whenever they look at the tassels, they remember the Commandments of God. (6)

3 The central feature of the synagogue is the ark, which contains the Sefer Torah and other scrolls. In front of it is placed a menorah. In the middle of the synagogue is the bimah or reading desk where the Sefer Torah is placed during worship. In Orthodox synagogues, men and women sit separately; women might sit in a gallery. (6)

4 The ark is at the front of the synagogue and contains the Torah Scroll and other scrolls. An eight-branched candlestick is placed near it and reminds the people of God's presence. The bimah is in the middle of the synagogue and it is where the Torah is read. There are seats on both sides. (6)

5 In the synagogue, men and boys cover their heads and everyone dresses modestly. The service is led by a rabbi in Hebrew for Orthodox Jews. It begins with saying psalms, followed by readings from the Torah and the prophets. There is usually a sermon followed by prayers. The service ends with kiddush. (6)

5.5 Orthodox and Reform Judaism

1 Orthodox and Reform Jews both believe that God alone must be worshipped. Both use the Torah for worship. Only Orthodox Jews believe it was revealed to Moses, which is why it must be read in Hebrew. Reform Jews worship using a mixture of Hebrew and English. Reform Jews allow women to become rabbis and women may wear the tallit. (6)

2 Orthodox Jews believe that God wrote the Torah and gave Moses the Oral Torah. The Torah cannot be changed. They believe that kosher laws should be kept strictly. Men and women have specific roles and may not sit together in synagogue. Men have more laws to fulfil in the community and women have more at home. (6)

3 Orthodox Jews take a traditional approach because they believe God is the author of the Torah but Reform Jews take a more liberal approach and say different people wrote it at different times. Because Orthodox Jews say God wrote it, they believe it cannot be changed. Reform Jews say it can be adapted for modern times. (6)

4 In the nineteenth century, changes in society meant that many Jews felt that Judaism needed to be reformed. This is how Reform Judaism started. Reform Jews say it is important to understand Torah in one's own language and that women as well as men may become rabbis. Orthodox Jews believe that as God's word does not change, then these reforms are unnecessary. (6)

5 Reform Jews believe that Judaism should be kept up to date with the modern world and adapted to fit science and social changes. They argue that the Torah was not revealed to Moses but to a number of people over a period of time. This is why some of its commandments are not necessary today, such as all the kosher laws. (6)

5.6 Family life

1 Kosher means that food is lawful to eat. If meat is eaten, it must be drained of all blood. It is not permitted to eat meat and dairy products together. Jews may eat fish, providing it has fins and scales, and meat, providing the animal has cloven hooves and eats grass. (6)

2 Home is a special place in Jewish life because it is where parents teach their children about their faith. Fathers help their children to study the Torah. Many rituals take place in the home, such as Shabbat when families share a special meal. The fact that a Jewish home is marked by a mezuzah also shows its importance. (6)

3 Women in the Jewish tradition must make sure the family is fed according to the food kosher kashrut laws. She must take care that her children and husband wear the right clothes, which are modest and comply with the Torah. She must prepare the house for the Sabbath and teach her daughters how to run their homes in the future. (6)

4   Men wear a kippah for all religious activities. This shows respect for God. They also wear two prayer boxes – tefillin – which contain the Shema. They wear one on their arm and one on their forehead as a reminder that God is one. They wear a tallit, which has tassels at each corner reminding them of all God's commandments.   (6)

5   Every Jewish home has a mezuzah on the right-hand side of every door in the house except for the bathroom. The mezuzah is a part of the Shema written on a piece of parchment. Wherever a person goes in their house, they see the mezuzah and are reminded to keep the commandments.   (6)

5.7 Shabbat

1   On Friday evening the father and older children attend synagogue. At home, the mother lights the candles and says the special prayer. When the father returns, kiddush is made over the wine and the hallot bread is blessed. On the Shabbat morning, the whole family attends synagogue. Children may attend religion school. The Shabbat ends with the lighting of the havdalah candle.   (6)

2   The mother and children clean and prepare the house. Then the mother lights the Shabbat candles, places her hands over her face and says a special blessing just before sunset. Then the father says kiddush over the wine and a blessing is made over two hallot loaves. When the meal is finished, the family sings Jewish songs.   (6)

3   In preparation for Shabbat, the women and children clean the house and make it tidy. They get the meal ready and lay the table with flowers and the best plates and glasses. The wine is uncorked and the candlesticks are polished. When everything is ready, the mother lights the candles and says a special blessing before sunset.   (6)

4   When the father and older boys return home, members of the family wish each other 'Shabbat shalom'. The father says kiddush, which is a blessing, over the wine. He also says a blessing over the two hallot loaves. These are distributed round the family. He recites some verses from the Tenach. The Sabbath meal is then eaten.   (6)

5   The mother lights candles on the Shabbat because light is a symbol of the presence of God. It is different from electric light and symbolises peace coming into the house. Saying kiddush over the wine and a blessing over the two specially baked hallot loaves is a reminder of God's love and generosity.   (6)

5.8 Birth and Bar Mitzvah

1   A year before a boy is 13 or a girl is 12, each goes to classes to learn about their responsibilities as a Jew. They also learn in Hebrew the portion of Torah they will read out in synagogue on the day of their Bar or Bat Mitzvah. Usually there are lots of relatives there and afterwards a party is given.   (6)

2   Becoming Bar Mitzvah means being recognised as an adult under the Jewish Law. This means setting a good example by following the commandments (or mitzvoth) prescribed for a man (or woman if Bat Mitzvah). For a boy, this means he is now entitled to wear a tallit and tefillin.   (6)

3   On the eighth day after the birth of a boy, he must be circumcised. This can take place in the synagogue or at home. His godfather holds him whilst the mohel carries out the operation.

The boy is given his Hebrew name as well as his ordinary name. A kiddush takes place with a blessing over a cup of wine. (6)

4   When boys are Bar Mitzvah they know that they are now recognised as adults in the Jewish community and therefore have a duty to carry out the relevant commandments (the mitzvoth) of the Torah responsibly. They must set a good example. They may now also wear tefillin and tallit. (6)

5   When a boy is born, a mohel, who is a pious Jew and skilled in circumcisions, carries out the operation at home or in the synagogue. The child is given his Hebrew name and a kiddush blessing is said over a cup of wine, and sometimes a drop of wine is placed on the baby's lips. (6)

5.9 From marriage to death

1   It is traditional for the couple to marry under a canopy or huppah. The bride and groom are led there by their respective families. Then the bride circles the groom. A special blessing is made over a cup of wine, from which the couple sips and a glass is broken by stepping on it. The rabbi reads from the marriage contract and then recites the seven blessings. (6)

2   The huppah is a canopy under which the bride and groom are married. The rabbi makes a blessing over a cup of wine, from which the bride and groom sip. The ketubah (or marriage contract) sets out the duties of the married couple. It is traditional for the bridegroom to crush some glass with his foot as sign of what God has yet in store for the future. (6)

3   After the burial of the body, everyone symbolically washes their hands as a sign of purity. The bereaved family stays at home for a week so friends and relatives can visit. They can bring food and comfort to the bereaved. A special prayer called the kaddish is said in the synagogue for the departed by the bereaved. (6)

4   In an Orthodox funeral the body is buried, whereas for Reform Jews the body may be cremated. The funeral should take place as soon after death as possible but not on the Shabbat. The body is dressed in a simple white garment (if it is a man, it may be his tallit). After the burial, mourners wash their hands. (6)

5   When an Orthodox Jew dies, the body is prepared for burial (not cremation). The body is cleansed and dressed in a white cloth. Although a funeral should take place as quickly as possible, time has to be given for relatives to travel. It is a blessing or mitzvah to attend the burial. Afterwards, during the period of shiva, relatives visit and give comfort to the mourners. (6)

5.10 Festivals

1   The festival of Hanukkah takes place during winter and remembers the time when Judas Maccabee won a great victory over the Greeks and then cleansed the Temple. Readings of the story take place, and to remember the miracle of the menorah the Hanukkah lamp is lit each day for eight days. It is a time for giving and receiving presents. Oily foods are eaten. (6)

2   The festival of Sukkot happens in the autumn. Jews remember their wanderings in the Sinai desert when they lived in shelters or sukkot. Now, they live in shelters for eight days, visit their friends and remember their dependence on God. In the synagogue they wave bundles of palm, myrtle, willow and citrus fruit, representing four aspects of humans in unity. (6)

3   Jews celebrate their new year (Rosh Hashanah) by remembering God's creation of the world. A ram's horn is blown at the beginning and end of the ten-day festival. People apologise to each other and ask for forgiveness. They have a special meal, starting with bread dipped in honey. The last day is Yom Kippur, when they attend synagogue, fast and repent.   (6)

4   The festival of Simchat Torah celebrates the moment when the weekly readings of the Torah that year have been completed. The last chapter of Deuteronomy is read followed immediately by Genesis 1. The Sefer Torah is then paraded round the inside of the synagogue seven times – the congregation follows, singing and dancing.   (6)

5   Festivals are important because they mark the seasons of the year and remind Jews of significant events in their history. For example, at Passover they remember the Exodus from Egypt and at Shavuot they remember when Moses received the Torah at Mount Sinai. The celebrations contain special symbols that keep alive the old stories and remind them of God's promises.   (6)

6   Once the house is cleared of all yeast products the seder begins, with the youngest person of the family asking four questions. The questions ask why this night is different from all other nights. Then everyone joins in the answer which is given in the Passover haggadah. At various moments in the answer four cups of wine are drunk and matzos is dipped into bitter herbs and haroset. Then the main meal is eaten, followed by everyone singing traditional songs.   (6)

7   Purim takes place in late February or early March. It celebrates the time when Queen Esther saved the Jews from the wicked Haman. During the synagogue service the story is read out from the Esther Scroll and every time Haman's name is mentioned the congregation make a lot of noise to blot out his name. Children dress up in costumes and bring rattles and whistles to add to the noise.   (6)

8   Shavuot takes place fifty days after Passover and has three main purposes. Firstly, it remembers the time when Moses received the Torah at Mount Sinai. So it's a time of thanksgiving. Secondly, it is also a harvest festival and a time for thanking God for the creation and His gifts to the world. Thirdly, it celebrates the gift of freedom which was gained after the Jews escaped from Egypt.   (6)

6 Islam

6.1 God

1 Muslims believe that there is only one God and there are no others. Allah is the creator of everything and everything that happens is due to His will. Only God may be worshipped and prayed to. God has 99 names. He is the Merciful and the Compassionate. At the end of time, He will judge all people according to their deeds. (6)

2 One of Allah's names is 'The Creator'. He created the universe, and all life and beauty come from Him. Another name is 'The All-Knowing' because He knows everything, from grand things in the universe to what is in a person's heart. He is called 'The Merciful', from the Arabic word for 'womb', showing how Allah offers life-giving care. (6)

3 God is creator because everything that exists is due to His will and everything that happens is the result of His will. This means there are no other gods who control the world and so only God must be worshipped. As God is creator of the universe, He is much greater than any single part of it. (6)

4 God is often associated with light because when Muhammad first experienced God in the cave called Hira, he experienced God as light. Angels are also considered to be light and God's message was revealed to Muhammad by Gabriel. Of all Allah's 99 beautiful names, light best expresses that God is sublime. (6)

5 As God is the creator of everything, He controls everything at all times. No human being could ever manage to live according to God's will, but God is merciful and is generous to those who try to live according to His will. He is also just. Everyone will be judged according to their deeds on the Day of Judgement. (6)

6.2 Muhammad

1 Muhammad was born in 570 C.E. When he was 40, the angel Gabriel appeared to him and God's words were revealed to him. He preached the oneness of God to the people of Makkah and then set up the first Muslim community at Madinah in 622 C.E. In 630 C.E. he returned to Makkah and removed the idols from the Ka'bah. (6)

2 Muhammad regularly prayed in a cave outside Makkah. In 610 C.E. the angel Gabriel appeared to him and told him to 'recite'. Muhammad refused three times and Gabriel squeezed him three times until suddenly he recited God's words. He was greatly shocked but was looked after by Khadijah, his wife, who became one of the first converts to Islam. (6)

3 Muhammad was born in 570 C.E. His parents died when he was young and he was therefore brought up by an uncle, Abu Talib, for whom he worked. He was a hard and honest worker and impressed a local businesswoman called Khadijah. She employed him and then, when he was 25, they married. (6)

4   Muhammad's message in Makkah was that God is one. He therefore told the Makkans not to worship any other gods and their idols. He told them that at judgement day God would know who had worshipped Him and who had not. This made the merchants very angry and they tortured and killed some of Muhammad's companions.   (6)

5   The people of Yathrib learned that Muhammad was very good at settling disputes. So they asked him to come to their city and sort out their arguments. In 622 C.E. Muhammad sent his family to live there. This is called the hijra. He quickly gained the trust of the people and he built his first mosque there. The town was renamed Madinah and became the first Muslim community.   (6)

6.3 Qur'an and Hadith

1   Muhammad received his first revelation of the Qur'an when he was in the Hira cave. Over the next 23 years, he received more revelations, which were written down by various people and stored in a box. However, after Muhammad's death, various versions were produced and Abu Bakr ordered that a standard copy should be made.   (6)

2   The Hadith is a collection of the sayings and actions of Muhammad. It is very important as it provides Muslims with examples of the Sunnah of the Prophet. This means Muslims are able to see how Muhammad behaved in various situations and can help explain how he understood the Qur'an.   (6)

3   Muslims believe that the Qur'an is the word of God as revealed to Muhammad by the angel Gabriel. They believe it was revealed to Muhammad over a period of 23 years. God sent him appropriate revelations when the situation required it. It is the final revelation of God, and Muslims believe it is the ultimate book of guidance.   (6)

4   The Qur'an is very important to Muslims because it is the actual word of Allah as revealed to Muhammad by the angel Gabriel. Qur'an means 'recitation'. This is why a true Qur'an can only be read in Arabic, its original language. Because it is the final word of God, it is perfect and its guidance is therefore of great importance.   (6)

5   Because the Qur'an is God's word, it must be given a lot of respect. When it is not being used it must be wrapped up and stored on a high shelf. In worship it must be kept off the ground and sometimes placed on a little desk or kursi. Before reading from it a person must wash.   (6)

6.4 Beliefs

1   The prophets are important in Islam because each delivers God's revelations at a particular time to a particular people. They are also examples of the ways in which a Muslim should submit to the will of Allah. Abraham, for example, was prepared to sacrifice his son Ishmael when God ordered him to do so.   (6)

2   The Five Pillars are the central duties every Muslim must perform. The first is to proclaim that there is only one God and Muhammad is His messenger. The second is to pray five times a day. The third is to give Zakah to help the poor. The fourth is to fast during Ramadan. The final duty is to go on Hajj.   (6)

3   On the Day of Judgement when the last trumpet is sounded, God will judge everyone's life according to their good and bad deeds. A record is kept by each person's guardian angels. The good will be given a place in Paradise and the wicked and unbelievers will be sent to Hell and a life of torment.   (6)

4   Because God is the creator of the world and there are no other gods, then God controls or wills everything that happens. As God is all-knowing He not only wills what is happening now but also what is yet to happen. This means although things may seem unfair to us, there is always a reason for everything. (6)

5   Angels are God's messengers. They are made of light but can take on human form when they need to communicate God's will to people. Usually they cannot be seen. They keep a record of everyone's good and evil deeds – even intended good deeds. At the end of prayer, a Muslim turns to his guardian angels on his left and right. (6)

6.5 Salah

1   Prayer is important to Muslims because it helps them remember Allah and keeps them from doing bad things. It is so important that it forms the second Pillar of Islam and has to be performed five times a day. Prayer enables people to off-load their worries and ask forgiveness, reminding them that they are dependent on their creator. (6)

2   Before praying, Muslims must ensure that they are modestly dressed. Everyone must perform wudu, which is a special sequence of washing one's hands, mouth, nose, face, arms, neck, ears and feet. Performing wudu is necessary to get oneself into the right frame of mind for prayer. The place for prayer must be clean. (6)

3   Muslims pray by facing towards the sacred Ka'bah in Makkah. They make sure that the place where they are praying is clean and therefore use a prayer rug. Before starting, they should wash themselves according to the rules of wudu. Prayer consists of a series of special movements or rakat, including putting one's head on the ground. (6)

4   In the mosque, men and women should sit apart, although women are encouraged to pray at home rather than the mosque. This is so there can be no distractions. Everyone prays towards the Ka'bah. Men and women prepare themselves in the same way through wudu and use almost the same prayer movements or rakat. (6)

5   Wudu is performed when preparing to pray at home or in the mosque. A Muslim first says a prayer praising Allah as being the most merciful and then he washes his hands, mouth, nose, face and arms each three times. Then he passes his hands over his hair. Finally he washes his ears, neck and feet. (6)

6.6 Mosque

1   The muezzin is the person who calls Muslims to prayer. He does this from the minaret in the mosque prior to each of the five prayer times. The call to prayer is called the adhan and it says that God is the greatest and Muhammad is His prophet. He calls the people to prayer facing towards the Ka'bah. (6)

2   Before going into a mosque, Muslims must ensure that they are modestly dressed. Everyone must perform wudu, which is a special sequence of washing one's hands, mouth, nose, face, arms, neck, ears and feet. Shoes are left outside the mosque so that dust and dirt are not brought into the prayer hall. (6)

3   In a typical mosque you will see the washroom or a fountain for wudu. There will be rooms for study and meetings. In the main prayer hall there will be the mihrab or niche and nearby the minbar or pulpit, from which the imam preaches and leads the worship. There might be a gallery or separate room for women to pray. (6)

4   The mihrab is an alcove in the kiblah wall and marks the direction of prayer towards the Ka'bah. The minbar is the pulpit from which the imam gives his sermon. The prayer hall is the large open space for worshippers and must be clean. There are many abstract patterns as God must not be represented in any figurative way. (6)

5   The adhan is the call to prayer. It is usually sung from a minaret by the muezzin. It contains the Shahadah or first Pillar of Faith. It tells people to come to prayer to bear witness that God is the greatest and that there is only one God. It also states that Muhammad is Allah's messenger. (6)

6.7 Zakah

1   Zakah is the third Pillar of Faith of Islam. It is a Muslim's duty as an act of worship to give 2.5 per cent of savings to the poor and needy, or hospitals, schools and mosques. It is paid secretly once a year and ensures a person is not selfish or greedy with their money. (6)

2   Zakah is very important for Muslims. Firstly, it is a reminder that everything belongs to God and that humans are stewards, not owners, of their wealth. Secondly, it reminds them not to be selfish but to be generous. Thirdly, it is an act worship to praise God. Finally, it is to help the poor and needy. (6)

3   Zakah is the third Pillar of Faith. It is a duty of Muslims to give to those less fortunate than themselves. It reminds them that as everything belongs to God, it is not theirs to keep. It is also a test to make sure they are not selfish. It must be given in secret so that the person doesn't get false praise from others. (6)

4   Zakah is given to a range of charities, for example newly converted Muslims, prisoners of war, hospitals and schools. By giving to the poor and needy, Muslims remember that everything they have belongs to Allah. As it is an act of worship, the giver also benefits by being closer to Allah. Everyone benefits from helping to create a fairer society. (6)

5   Traditionally, Zakah must be given in secret. This is because it must be done in praise of God and not to gain the praise of others. The amount given varies. For farmers it must be at least five per cent of their crops and animals. In Muslim countries, the government can collect Zakah as tax. (6)

6.8 Sawm

1   During Ramadan it is a duty of all those who can to fast during the day. Fasting, or Sawm, is the fourth Pillar of Islam and it is a time when Muslims can think about their spiritual life and appreciate the good things God provides. Suffering hunger is a test of obedience. After sunset, Muslims may break the fast. (6)

2   During Ramadan, Muslims fast during the daylight hours, starting from just before dawn to just after sunset. During this time, there must be no eating or chewing of food, smoking or making love. The whole of the Qur'an is recited and Muslims are encouraged to listen to or to read as much of it as possible. (6)

3   Fasting is important because it is an act of worship. It reminds Muslims of their dependence on God who is the creator and provider of everything. It makes them obedient to God's commands and their duties to Him. It makes them aware of those who are less fortunate than themselves – the poor and weak. (6)

4   During Ramadan, everyone fasts and the whole of the Qur'an is recited. On one day towards the end of Ramadan, the Night of Power is celebrated. This is the time when Muhammad received his first revelation from God and it is traditional for Muslims to stay awake for the whole of the night and offer special prayers. (6)

5   Everyone is expected to fast during Ramadan, but if fasting would cause harm then it is not a duty. For example, someone who is sick need not fast. Mothers who are breastfeeding their children do not need to fast. Children under the age of twelve are excused and so are very old people. (6)

6.9 Hajj

1   Muslims go on Hajj because it is a duty for adult Muslims to go at least once in their lifetime. It is the fifth Pillar of Faith. Hajj is an opportunity to meet over 2 million Muslims and experience umma – unity. They carry out the actions in Makkah that Muhammad laid down. It is also a time for prayer, reflection and repentance. (6)

2   Before Muslims arrive in Makkah they change into simple white clothes. They circle the Ka'bah seven times and run between the two hills and the Zamzam well. Then they camp out overnight at Mina and then move on to the Plain of Arafat. The stay out overnight at Muzdafilah and then once they have visited the pillars of Mina they return back to Makkah. (6)

3   The first moment is putting oneself into a state of ihram (spiritual purity) and then circling the Ka'bah seven times. The next moment is standing in the Plain of Arafat in front of God to make one's confession and ask for forgiveness. The final moment is throwing stones at the pillars of Mina to drive out Satan. (6)

4   When a pilgrim arrives in Makkah, his first action is to circle the holy Ka'bah seven times. Then he runs between the two hills and the Zamzam well. The next day he sets off for the Plain of Arafat to pray and meditate. The following day he goes to the pillars of Mina where he throws stones to drive out Satan. (6)

5   The Ka'bah is the shrine that Muhammad circled seven times, so pilgrims do the same. The Zamzam well reminds pilgrims of the time when Hagar was desperate and found water in the wilderness. The Plain of Arafat provides a time of prayer and repentance, and the pillars of Mina remind pilgrims how Abraham had to resist Satan. (6)

6.10 Birth and death

1   When a person dies, their body is washed and anointed. It is then wrapped in white sheets – three for a man and five for a woman. Burial should take place as quickly as possible. The body is buried with the person's face orientated towards the Ka'bah. Passages from the Qur'an are recited as earth is thrown into the grave. (6)

2   First, the father whispers the adhan into the baby's right ear. Then he rubs a piece of date or honey on the baby's gums to wish it a sweet life. Seven days later its head is shaved, the hair weighed and the equivalent weight in money is given to the poor. The baby is named and a party is given. (6)

3   Aqiqah takes place seven days after the birth of a Muslim child. The child's head is shaved and sometimes the hair's weight is then given in equivalent money to the poor. The child is given a name, which can be one of God's 99 names. Then there is a party for family and friends. (6)

4 When a person dies, their body is washed, anointed and wrapped in white sheets. Burial should take place as soon after death as possible. Bodies are buried with their face facing towards the Ka'bah. Words from the Qur'an are recited. Seven days later relatives return to the grave to remember the three gifts the deceased has left: helpful possessions, knowledge and example to his children. (6)

5 Muslims believe that after the Day of Judgement, when God judges everyone according to their deeds, Paradise will follow and everyone will meet up again. That is why, although death is a sad occasion, Muslims know it is not the end. They also believe a good person will have contributed wealth and knowledge to others. (6)

6.11 Marriage

1 Everyone wears their best clothes. The ceremony can take place at home or in the mosque. Two witnesses need to be present when the marriage contract is signed. Then various passages from the Qur'an are recited and the couple is considered to be husband and wife. The following day the bridegroom gives a large party for all the wedding guests. (6)

2 Marriage is very important because it is the bedrock of family life and a stable society. The Qur'an encourages couples to marry. Marriage is the means of giving rights to men and women, and the way to protect each other's rights in the event of divorce. Husbands must provide for their wives and treat them with great respect. (6)

3 Arranged marriages take place in Islam because love is not the primary reason for getting married. The first reason is for companionship and having children. Love follows later. That is why parents, who have more experience of life, are often in a better position to know who would suit their child best. Children must agree to their parents' choice. (6)

4 Marriage is important for Muslims because Muhammad married several times and many of the prophets before him were married. Marriage is the place where Muslim values such as respect, generosity and mercy can be taught by example. A husband must provide for his wife and respect her rights. A wife has duties to look after her husband and children. (6)

5 A man may marry up to four wives if his first wife gives her permission and it is permitted by the law of the country where the Muslim is living. Sex may only take place in marriage; sex before or outside marriage is very wrong. Divorce is allowed as a last resort. A wife keeps her dowry if this happens. (6)

6.12 Family life

1 Children must respect their parents by being obedient to them (and also to their other adult relatives). Children should never cause deliberate harm to their parents and in their old age it is the duty of children to care for their parents until they die. This might mean children having their parents live with them in their home. (6)

2 In a Muslim family, parents have to set an example to their children and be kind to them. They must feed, clothe and educate them without favouritism. Parents should never harm their children. Parents have a responsibility to bring them up as good Muslims. If their own parents are alive, they must show them respect. (6)

3 Parents have duties to their children. They must be kind and fair and set a good example to their children. They must treat all their children equally and not have favourites. They must never cause their children deliberate harm. They must provide them with education, a home and protection. (6)

4 Children must be obedient to their parents. They must respect them and never cause them intentional harm. They have special duties to look after them in their old age, just as they were looked after when they were young. They should also give respect to their grandparents and relatives. They must work hard at school and be law-abiding. (6)

5 In a typical Muslim family, a father will be the primary bread-winner and provide the material needs of his wife and children. A mother will ensure that the children are fed, clothed and educated. Both parents will teach their children to respect them and their elders. Children will work hard at school and learn to respect the law. (6)

6.13 Festivals

1 Id-ul-Fitr marks the end of Ramadan when Muslims have been fasting. People dress up in their best clothes and children are given presents. It is a time for giving a special Zakah to the poor. Many go to the mosque to pray and then a special meal is eaten at midday. It is a holiday so no work is done. (6)

2 Id-ul-Fitr takes place at the end of Ramadan. People dress up in their best clothes, children are given presents and a special midday meal is eaten. It is traditional to give a special Zakah to the poor. Id-ul-Adha takes place towards the end of the Hajj period. An animal is sacrificed and a meal is shared with friends, family and the poor. (6)

3 Id-ul-Adha takes place towards the end of the Hajj and also takes place for those not on Hajj. It remembers when Abraham was tempted by Satan not to listen to God's command. Because Abraham was faithful to God he was commanded to sacrifice an animal. At the festival, an animal is sacrificed and then a meal is shared with friends, family and the poor. (6)

4 Muslims remember Abraham's near sacrifice of Ishmael to Allah and how he was told by an angel to sacrifice a ram instead. At the festival of Id-ul-Adha they remember this story as a symbol of their own willingness to give up their lives and possessions to Allah. They sacrifice an animal and then share the meat with the poor. (6)

7 Hinduism

7.1 Holy books

1   Hindu holy books fall into two types: sruti and smritis. The sruti books are the ancient books, the Vedas. They provide knowledge of the world and are believed to come from God. The Rig Veda is the most important. There are also the Upanishads, which meditate on Brahman. The smritis include the Mahabharata and the Ramayana.   (6)

2   The story is about two families, the Kurus and Pandavas. Pandu becomes king but he wants to be a holy man so he gives his kingdom and children (the Pandavas) to his brother to look after. But his brother's children (the Kurus) try to kill the Pandavas. Pandu's brother gives the Pandavas half the kingdom but the Kurus steal it. In a great battle that follows the Pandavas win it back.   (6)

3   The Vedas are the most important holy books of the Hindus. They are written in Sanskrit, although originally they were learned by heart. There are four books of the Vedas, of which the most popular is the Rig Veda. The Vedas include hymns to the deities. The smritis are explanations of the Vedas, often through stories such as the Ramayana.   (6)

4   The Upanishads are sruti. They mean literally 'to sit at the feet of' and are discussions between teachers and pupils about the ideas contained in the Vedas. They are in the form of poems written by holy men and meditate on important ideas such as Brahman and its relationship with atman. There are over 200 Upanishads.   (6)

5   The story is about cousins who go to war over who should be the next king. Prince Arjuna does not want to fight his relations so he asks Krishna, who is acting as his chariot driver, for advice. Krishna says he should do his duty because his cousins have done wrong. He therefore fights and wins the battle.   (6)

7.2 Beliefs

1   Brahman refers to the eternal and invisible aspect of God. It is the origin of everything and the spirit of everything, invisible but greater. Atman is the soul or essence of a living being. It is part of Brahman and when someone dies their jivatman either moves into another body or merges into Brahman.   (6)

2   Atman refers to the soul or essence of every living being. Atman is also an aspect of Brahman, which means that humans can know Brahman because they know their atman. Samsara means reincarnation, so when a person dies their atman transfers to another body. Samsara also happens throughout life as our bodies change, but the atman remains the same.   (6)

3 Dharma means duty and doing what is morally right. It exists eternally and can be known through conscience, and through the reading of the Hindu scriptures such as the Vedas, Upanishads and the Bhagavad Gita. A person's duty also depends on what caste they belong to.   (6)

4 Ahimsa means non-violence. No one should deliberately harm a living being. This is because all living beings have atman, which is an aspect of Brahman. Therefore to harm a living being is causing harm to Brahman and brings about negative karma. Humans have a duty to look after nature, especially animals. The earth is 'our mother' and must be respected.   (6)

5 Karma means action and refers to the law of cause and effect. Every action that is performed has consequences, both good and bad. A good life means that the next life will be happier or better; a bad life will cause a less fortunate future life. Bad karma might mean a person is reborn in a lower life form.   (6)

7.3 Caste and dharma

1 Caste is the social group into which a person is born. Dharma means holy law and is a special duty, which depends partly on which caste you are born into. There are traditional jobs associated with each caste, so it is the duty of every member to carry out the job of his caste, such as the vaishyas who are skilled workers.   (6)

2 The caste system is the way society is divided up into varnas or classes. There are four varnas and each one is associated with particular tasks or jobs. It is therefore one's dharma to carry out these duties. The four varnas are: brahmins – priests and teachers; kshatriyas – rulers and warriors; vaishyas – farmers and traders; shudras – unskilled workers.   (6)

3 The four castes or varnas in Hinduism are: brahmins – priests and teachers; kshatriyas – rulers and warriors; vaishyas – skilled workers and traders; shudras – unskilled workers. Each varna has special duties associated with that caste and it is one's dharma or duty to carry them out. It is illegal in India today to discriminate against someone because of their caste.   (6)

4 Dharma means duty. Dharma refers to the invisible law of the universe, which governs how it operates. It is the Eternal Truth. But it also refers to the specific duties of each of the four varnas or castes. Carrying out one's dharma affects your karma for the future in this life and when reincarnated. Brahmins have duties as priests and as teachers.   (6)

5 Karma means action and refers to the law of cause and effect. Good actions have positive karmic effects and bring benefit in future lives. A person will know what is required of them depending on their caste or varna. For example, a vaishya knows as a trader that he has duties to trade fairly otherwise he will create bad karma.   (6)

7.4 Goal

1 Moksha is the goal of life and it means that a person is released from the cycle of rebirths or samsara. In order to achieve this, the atman or soul has to be purified. There are three paths to moksha: karma, or good works; understanding and knowledge, or jnana; and devotion to God, or bhakti.   (6)

2 People can achieve their goal in life in a number of ways. First they can carry out their dharma according to their caste (varna). This will create good karma and eventually release them from samsara. They can seek knowledge of jnana through meditation and understanding of existence. They can practise bhakti through love, devotion and worship of God.   (6)

3. The three paths to God are karma, jnana and bhakti. Karma means that God is active and we must offer our actions to him. Jnana means that God is the light of true knowledge to whom we should offer our minds. Bhakti means that God is love and must be worshipped. (6)

4. A Hindu might become free of samsara or the cycle of reincarnation by living a life that purifies atman so at death it can be released and become one with Brahman (God). This is called moksha. Traditionally there are three paths to moksha: karma, or good actions; jnana, or knowledge through meditation; and bhakti, or devotion to family and God. Raja yoga achieves moksha through bodily and mental control. (6)

5. Karma means being morally good by doing good works according to the dharma of one's caste. Jnana means knowledge of God by developing a calm mind through meditation. Bhakti means being loving and devoted to God and one's family. Any one or all three of these ways can lead to moksha and release from samsara. (6)

7.5 God

1. Many Hindus believe in only one God who is Brahman. As Brahman, God is the invisible spirit of the universe, sustaining all aspects of life. He has many aspects and so he can be worshipped in many different forms or gods. These different forms show that God is active and loves the world. (6)

2. Vishnu, the preserver of the cosmos, is symbolised as having four arms and holding a conch. He also has ten avatars, including a fish, a tortoise, Rama and Krishna. Shiva is often shown as a dancing figure. He holds a drum, dances inside a ring of fire and stands on a demon. (6)

3. Shiva is one of the manifestations of Brahman or the supreme form of God. He is shown in various ways. One of the most popular is as a dancer. His dance symbolises the power of creation and his drum symbolises the rhythm of life. The ring of fire that surrounds him shows he can create and destroy. (6)

4. The first path is karma, which means a person must be active and do good works and work hard to fulfil dharma. The second is jnana. This means training one's mind to know God and overcome the desires of the body. The third is bhakti, meaning to love and worship God through worship and devotion. (6)

5. Vishnu is one of the manifestations of Brahman or the supreme form of God. He is the preserver of the universe and his four arms symbolise his power. He holds a conch shell, which symbolises worship. Vishnu comes to earth in various forms or avatars. Six of these are animal forms and four human, including Rama and Krishna. (6)

7.6 From birth to death

1. When a baby is born, traditionally the priest or brahmin works out a horoscope to see how the planets are arranged and how these will affect that person's life. The horoscope will also tell the parents which letter their child's name should begin with. Some choose names of the deities such as Krishna or Lakshmi. (6)

2. Sometime between his eighth and eleventh birthday a boy goes through the ceremony when a thread of three strands and colours is placed over his left shoulder by a priest or teacher. He wears it for life to show that he is an adult. The priest explains his three duties are to God, his parents and his religious teachers. (6)

3 After the preparations for the wedding, the couple takes seven steps round a fire. The fire represents God's presence and this symbolises their hope for children and a happy life together. They carry a scarf to show that they are joined together, and on their last step they become husband and wife. Sometimes rice is sprinkled on the couple. (6)

4 Some men prepare for death in old age by going on pilgrimage or by becoming sanyasi – a wandering holy man. When Hindus die, their bodies are washed and dressed in new clothes and flowers are placed round them. In traditional funerals the body is cremated on a funeral pyre and the ashes are sprinkled in a holy river. This recognises that the atman has already begun its next stage. (6)

5 The body is first washed and then dressed in new clothes. Family and friends pay their respects by bringing flowers and touching the dead person's feet. The flowers are put around the body. Then it is traditional for the body to be cremated. The funeral pyre is lit by the eldest son and then the ashes are scattered. (6)

7.7 Pilgrimage

1 Pilgrimage to places such as the source of the River Ganges is important to Hindus because it is a religious duty. It is a way of showing endurance in order to worship God. It costs money, time and effort to go on pilgrimage. Every pilgrim accepts such difficulties for the sake of spiritual gain and cleansing. (6)

2 Hindus might go on pilgrimage to Jagannath in the city of Puri. Here there is a huge image of Krishna. At the festival of Jagannath, pilgrims pull a cart carrying Lord Jagannatha, who is a form of Krishna. Hundreds of thousands of pilgrims form the procession at the festival along with elephants and sadhus. (6)

3 Pilgrimage is a time of spiritual cleansing because it requires effort, concentration and devotion. Effort or the path of karma is required because some places are thousands of miles away. Concentration or jnana means being in the right frame of mind; pilgrimage is not just a social occasion. Finally devotion is shown by performing puja at the place of pilgrimage. (6)

4 Varanasi is important for Hindu pilgrims because it is the holy city situated on the river Ganges. The river Ganges is the most holy of all rivers because it is believed to wash away sins and make a person spiritually pure. Being in Varanasi with thousands of other pilgrims gives the pilgrim a very strong sense of being part of the Hindu faith. (6)

5 Pilgrims go to the Ganges because the river is considered to be sacred. The river brings pure water from the Himalayas and is thought to have been created by Shiva. Bathing in the waters washes away sins and enables the pilgrim to become pure. On the banks of the Ganges is Varanasi, where there are over a thousand temples. (6)

7.8 Festivals

1 Holi is a spring festival that celebrates the death of the evil Princess Holika. It is a time of practical jokes and lighting bonfires. Divali takes place in late autumn and lasts for several days. It remembers the time when Rama returned home having defeated Ravana. People light oil lamps and set off fireworks. (6)

2 Dassehra remembers the story of Rama. Many act out the story, which tells of the time when Sita was kidnapped by Ravana and found later by Hanuman. At the festival the great

battle between Ravana and Rama is re-enacted by making and smashing models of Ravana. Others light large images of Ravana filled with fireworks. (6)

3 Divali takes place in late autumn and lasts for several days. It remembers the time when Rama returned home having defeated Ravana. People light oil lamps and set off fireworks. Light symbolises the victory of good over evil and welcomes the goddess Lakshmi into people's homes. The story of Rama is read. (6)

4 The New Year festival is celebrated in March or April. Families make a banner, which they hang outside the front door of their houses. Some make Rangoli or special patterns outside their house. Holi is a spring festival that celebrates the death of the evil Princess Holika. It is a time of practical jokes and lighting bonfires. (6)

5 Festivals are important because they remind Hindus of the different seasons of the year and the great Indian heroes and events in history. It is a time for local communities to come together, for people to have fun and learn more about their faith. For example, Dassehra remembers how Rama defeated Ravana, and Holi celebrates spring and people play practical jokes. (6)

7.9 Worship at home

1 A shrine can be set up in a corner of a room or be a whole room. It will contain pictures and images (murti) of the family deities. Every day the deities are woken by lighting a lamp. The murti is washed and dressed. Flowers are offered and incense burned. Lastly, special food is offered and blessed. (6)

2 At home a person finds a quiet place to create a shrine, which contains an image (murti) to the deity. Worship begins by lighting candles; then the murti is dressed and offered food. Incense is burned. Before worship, a person washes or bathes and puts on clean clothes. In the temple, people ring a bell to announce themselves to the deity. (6)

3 Puja at home consists of waking up the deity each day and washing the murti and dressing it. Flowers and prashad or blessed food are offered (which is then eaten by the family). Prayers are recited, which might be a mantra, or others practise yoga or meditation. At night the murti is put away. (6)

4 Each household has its own favourite deity (or deities) whom it worships. The murti represents the deity and is treated with a great deal of respect. Each day the murti is woken up and a lamp is lit. Then it is washed and dressed. Flowers are offered and placed around the murti along with special blessed food. (6)

5 The lamp is used at the start of puja in the morning to wake the deity. The murti or image of the deity is washed and an offering of flowers is made. The specially blessed food that is offered to the deity is called prashad. During worship some prayers may be chanted; these are called mantras. (6)

7.10 Temple

1 Temples have huge spires or shikhara to represent the atman's journey from earth to moksha and the meeting of heaven and earth. The spires usually have carvings of animals, humans and deities on them. The porch contains the vehicle or vihara of the deity. Inside, there is a main hall or mandapa and the inner shrine, which contains the image of the deity. (6)

2   The priest's role is to look after the deity. He wakes up the deity in the morning and washes the murti. He offers it food, dresses it and makes it ready to be seen by worshippers. He performs arti and blows the conch shell at the start and end of the ceremony. Finally he prepares the murti for the night. (6)

3   The spire symbolises the journey of the atman to moksha or release from samsara. The carvings of animals, humans and deities symbolise how Brahman is part of every aspect of existence. The vihara is found in the porch and is the vehicle of the deity. The inner shrine contains the image of the deity. (6)

4   The priest rings the bell to wake the deity and to announce to worshippers that it is now ready for prayers. People worship in groups or meditate by themselves. The scriptures are read and then the priest performs arti. Offerings of incense, fire and water are made and worshippers offer money, food and flowers. Then the priest distributes prashad. (6)

5   Arti is when the priest passes round a lamp and each person circles their hands around it. The fire symbolises the presence of God or Brahman. The ceremony of arti takes place before the other offerings of money, food and flowers. The priest blows a conch shell before and after the ceremony. (6)

8 Buddhism

8.1 Siddhartha

1 Siddhartha was born into a rich family and his father was a ruler of a clan in North India. He was trained in martial arts and married when he was 16. When he was born, a wise man said he would grow up to be a religious teacher. His father did everything he could to make sure he didn't come into contact with the outside world. (6)

2 When Siddhartha was a child, a wise man said he would grow up to become a religious teacher. But his father wanted Siddhartha to follow him and become a ruler. He thought that if he removed everything that might cause Siddhartha to think about religious ideas, such as suffering and death, then the prophecy would not come true. (6)

3 Siddhartha's father, Shuddhodana, made sure that in his palace his son would only experience good things and luxuries. He hoped that his son would naturally wish to follow him as ruler. He made sure that in the palace anyone suffering from illness or who was dying was removed. (6)

4 When Siddhartha was born, there were many extraordinary signs that he would grow up to be a wise man. When he was a child, everyone recognised him as being exceptionally kind and generous. During this time, Asita predicted that Siddhartha would grow up to be a religious leader. To stop this, his father made him marry early and gave him a life of luxury. (6)

5 Although Siddhartha lived a life of luxury and was married with a child, he was not happy. His father had stopped him from seeing the outside world because he didn't want him to be anything other than a ruler. But Siddhartha felt that he was missing some important experiences of life and he wanted to see life outside the palace. (6)

8.2 Siddhartha's quest

1 Siddhartha asked Channa, his chariot driver, to take him out secretly into the town so he could see life as it was really lived. He saw four sights: an old person, a sick person, a dead person and a holy man. He was impressed by the holy man so he left the palace and for six years became an ascetic. (6)

2 Siddhartha was not happy with his life of luxury in the palace. In the town he saw four sights: sickness, old age, death and a wandering holy man. He therefore left the palace and became an ascetic, joining five other ascetics. For six years he ate almost nothing and meditated. (6)

3 The first thing Siddhartha saw was an old person. The second thing was a sick person and the third was a dead body. These things made him realise that everyone grows old and dies and that everything changes. The fourth sight was of a holy man who had given up earthly possessions to live a spiritual life. (6)

4   As an ascetic Siddhartha would fast for long periods of time. During this time he would meditate and practise extreme yogic exercises such as breath control, and eat a few grains of wheat. He did this for six years. He grew very thin and almost died. As he didn't achieve enlightenment he decided to stop being an ascetic. (6)

5   Siddhartha began his quest because although he was happily married, his life of luxury was not enough. Deep down he knew that this life was superficial and he was not seeing it as it really is. So when he saw the four sights of suffering and death, he knew that he needed to find another way to seek contentment. (6)

8.3 The Enlightened One

1   The Buddha had visions of his past lives and of the suffering he had been through. The god Mara tried to stop him meditating by tempting him sexually by offering him his daughters. But then he realised the Three Great Knowledges. Firstly, knowledge of his previous lives; secondly, everything is controlled by karma; thirdly, the Four Noble Truths. (6)

2   When Siddhartha sat under the Bodhi tree he said he would stay there for as long as it took to achieve enlightenment. At night he experienced many temptations and had visions of his previous lives and Mara's daughters tempting him. Then at dawn he felt he had achieved enlightenment and gained knowledge over the obstacles of craving, hatred, fear and doubt. (6)

3   Siddhartha's temptations were very powerful. He was tempted sexually. The god Mara offered him beautiful women to try and distract him from his meditation with visions of death and sexual desires. By focusing his mind on the morning star he was able to overcome the temptations and achieve enlightenment. (6)

4   Siddhartha's life with the five ascetics had not produced enlightenment. When he decided to eat and give up being an ascetic, they left him. Siddhartha decided to sit under the Bodhi tree and to stay there and meditate until he discovered the truth. He was tempted by the god Mara and experienced the suffering in all his previous lives. (6)

5   Siddhartha became the Buddha when he realised three things about knowledge. First that he had many previous lives. The second was that he saw how people's many previous lives and deaths are governed by their actions. The third was the Four Noble Truths of dukkha, tanha, nirodha and the Noble Eightfold Path. (6)

8.4 Dharma

1   Karma means intentional action and describes the universal law of cause and effect. Every action has consequences now, in the future and in future lives. At rebirth karma determines what kind of existence you are born into. By following the Noble Eightfold Path a person may overcome bad habits from previous lives and achieve merit (punna karma). (6)

2   The Four Noble Truths teach that all life involves suffering or dukkha. This suffering is caused by an unhealthy desire or tanha for earthly things like pleasure and money. Suffering can be overcome (nirodha) if a person can stop their harmful desires. The fourth truth is the Middle Way or Noble Eightfold Path. (6)

3   The Three Universal Truths are anicca, anatta and dukkha. The First Truth is that everything changes. This is called anicca. The Second Truth is that we don't have souls; we are made up of a number of elements. This is called anatta. The Third Truth is that there is suffering in the world. This is called dukkha. (6)

4   The Noble Eightfold Path is the fourth part of the Four Noble Truths. This is the Middle Way between the extreme of finding enlightenment by fasting and by living a life of luxury. The Noble Eightfold Path says that we should adopt the right intentions to train the mind by practising right speech, livelihood, effort, etc. (6)

5   Nirvana is not a place like heaven. It is a state of mind, which is achieved when a person stops desiring or craving things or experiencing the Three Poisons (or fires) of ignorance, hatred and greed. It means 'blowing out' all these desires and is a state of freedom, joy and contentment. (6)

8.5 Sangha

1   The sangha is the worldwide Buddhist community. It gives support to those gaining enlightenment. It can also refer more specifically to the communities of monks and nuns. Monks and nuns have special duties and are further along the path of enlightenment. One duty is the teaching and study of the dharma. (6)

2   The role of monks and nuns in Buddhism is to seek enlightenment through meditation and the carrying out of the dharma. They do this through study and teaching of the dharma. They teach each other and also lay people. They have many rules to follow, which include wearing a simple robe and avoiding all luxuries. (6)

3   The sangha is important because it is one of the Three Refuges. It represents the community of Buddhists worldwide. It is the means of giving support to all those seeking enlightenment and living according to the Noble Eightfold Path. For example, in exchange for the teaching of the dharma from monks and nuns, lay people offer them food. (6)

4   Belonging to the sangha helps a person live a good life because it means they have the support and encouragement of all other Buddhists. As a bhikkhu or a bhikkhuni, a person also has the discipline of living in a monastery and of keeping to the extra rules. They also study dharma more intensively. (6)

5   The first sangha was formed when the Buddha gathered together his first followers. He did not agree with the Indian caste system so the members of his community or sangha were all equals. The Buddha divided the sangha into monks and nuns. He gave them a special responsibility to teach the dharma. In time, they formed monasteries or viharas. (6)

8.6 Types of Buddhism

1   Mahayana is aimed at lay people and not just monks and nuns. There are many different forms of Mahayana Buddhism. One form is Pure Land Buddhism, which believes that by repeating Nembutsu a person can enter a perfect Buddha Land. Zen Buddhism teaches that everyone has a Buddha nature that can be found through being attentive to every action. (6)

2   Western Buddhism simply describes the way Buddhism mostly from China and India has spread in the West. Some forms of it have been especially adapted and modified to fit in with Western societies. For example, Triratna mix all three Buddhist traditions but do not have monks or nuns. (6)

3   Pure Land Buddhism is a form of Mahayana Buddhism. Its followers think that by chanting Nembutsu as a form of meditation they are keeping their minds focused on Amida Buddha. They believe Amida Buddha will help them overcome the Three Poisons and lead them into a pure state called Buddha Land. This place is perfect for practising the dharma.   (6)

4   Zen Buddhism became very popular in Japan. It teaches that everyone has a Buddha nature, which can be achieved through the training of the mind. This can be done through doing simple things with great concentration and mindfulness of everything that is going on. For example, having tea or arranging flowers can become part of Zen meditation.   (6)

5   Tibetan Buddhism is very colourful and flamboyant, while Theravada Buddhism is simple. Tibetan Buddhism encourages people to be involved in their religion in an active and imaginative way. They use wall hangings and images for meditation. In Theravada, Buddhists meditate away from distractions. Debate is common in Tibetan monasteries while quiet meditation is the focus of Theravada Buddhists.   (6)

8.7 Refuge

1   Going for refuge in the Buddha means becoming more Buddha-like in life. This means studying the Buddha's life and learning from the way he gave up his life of luxury to practise the Middle Way. Following the Buddha might mean choosing to become a monk or a nun.   (6)

2   The three refuges are: to go to the Buddha, to go to the dharma, to go to the sangha. The first means to follow the example of the Buddha and his life. The second means to study and learn from his teaching. The third means to become part of the worldwide community of Buddhists, either monastic or lay.   (6)

3   When a person has learned something of Buddhism and wishes to make Buddhism their way of life they make a solemn declaration. The declaration is made before an ordained Buddhist and the person says: 'I go to the Buddha for refuge. I go to the dharma for refuge. I go to the sangha for refuge.' They make offerings of candles, flowers and incense.   (6)

4   When a person has said the three refuges they make offerings of candles, flowers and incense. The light of the candles represents wisdom that the person will live by. The flowers represent beauty but also that everything changes because the flowers will soon fade and die. The incense represents the person's good deeds that will fill the world.   (6)

5   A person should spend some time learning about Buddhism and its practices before deciding to dedicate themselves to it for the rest of their lives. When they wish to make this moment official they say the three refuges in front of an ordained member of the sangha. They also promise to keep to the Five Precepts.   (6)

8.8 Buddha images

1   Buddha images are often quite different from each other. Some are the traditional Buddha seated or lying on his side, while others are brightly coloured and have many arms and legs. Others show what it would be like to be a Buddha in different stages of enlightenment, such as showing compassion. Tibetan Buddha images may express anger or determination.   (6)

2   The Buddha images may influence a person's life because they teach different aspects of Buddhism. For example, an image of an angry Buddha teaches that it is natural to become

angry but what matters is how that anger is directed to do good things. Images help a person to meditate. For example, the Amida Buddha depicts a state of calm. (6)

3   The flame is a symbol of the Buddha's enlightenment. The image of stepping down symbolises how a bodhisattva has chosen not to enter parinirvana but is using his wisdom to help others. The thunderbolt or vajra is a symbol of determination. (6)

4   A bodhisattva is an enlightened being who has decided not to enter into parinirvana but remain in the world to guide and inspire others. Images of bodhisattvas are used in meditation. For example, Avalokiteshvara is shown with many arms, symbolising compassion. Sometimes he is shown stepping down to symbolise how he helps people in the world. (6)

5   An image (or rupa) might be used to help reflect on the kind of person you are; an angry Buddha might help you deal with anger. An image of the historical Buddha as an ascetic might help you to reflect on the Buddha's teaching on craving. An image of a calm Buddha might help you to achieve the right frame of mind to meditate. (6)

8.9 Shrines, temples and monuments

1   A Buddhist shrine is often to be found in a person's home. It may have one or more Buddhist images. There is no set form of puja although it will include chanting, and making offerings of flowers, candles and incense. There might be reading from the Buddhist scriptures. A bell might be used to signal the next stage of puja. (6)

2   One image might be a rupa. A rupa is an image of the Buddha that depicts some aspects of Buddhist teaching. These rupas are intended to help a person in their meditation. Another symbol is the seven offering bowls. These bowls are placed in front of the rupa as if the Buddha is an honoured visitor coming from a journey. (6)

3   When a person enters a temple they might make an offering to the Buddha image (rupa) of flowers or fruit. At the shrine there will be seven bowls and incense. They then might listen to a passage from the Buddhist scriptures. They might join in with chanting. A bell is rung when the next stage of puja begins. (6)

4   A stupa is a monument set up to honour some aspect of the Buddha's life. Some contain a relic such as a piece of his clothing. Stupas are important for pilgrims as they are a focus of the Buddha's life and teaching. Pilgrims walk round a stupa several times out of respect for the Buddha. (6)

5   A typical shrine will have a rupa or Buddha image as its focus. In a temple, these can be vast. At home, it may be a small image placed on a table. Shrines can be in monasteries or a special area at home. Shrines often have cushions for meditation, seven offering bowls and a gong or bell. (6)

8.10 Festivals

1   There are few festivals in Buddhism because the Buddhist way of life is about achieving mindfulness and some think festivals can be distracting. Others find them helpful to remember the life and enlightenment of the Buddha (Wesak), his teaching (Full Moon), to remember the environment (New Year) and feeling part of the sangha. (6)

2   Pavarana Day takes place when the monks and nuns have completed Vassa. Each monk and nun confesses any faults he or she may have committed. Kathina takes place shortly afterwards and is the time when the lay people make a special dana to the monks and nuns, such as material for new robes. (6)

3   Wesak is the most important festival and is celebrated at the full moon in May. Buddhists remember the Buddha's birth in the palace, his enlightenment under the Bodhi tree and his death. Homes are often decorated with candles. There are processions in the streets and local shrines are specially decorated. (6)

4   Nirvana Day remembers the death of the Buddha when he achieved parinirvana. Buddhists go to temples and monasteries to meditate. It is a time of giving presents and to remember family and friends who may have died recently. (6)

5   Offerings are a means of acquiring merit or positive karma. Offerings include decorating shrines, especially at Wesak. At some New Year festivals, Buddha images are washed as a symbol of new life. At Kathina, gifts are made to the local monastery and new robes are given to the bhikkhus and bhikkhunis as dana and a sign of belonging to the sangha. (6)

8.11 Buddhist way of life

1   The environment must be protected for two reasons. Firstly, it is wrong to cause harm to any living being. We should always act out of loving kindness (metta) and compassion. Secondly, even the way we treat non-living things can affect living beings. The environment is not just for humans to use as they wish. (6)

2   The Five Precepts are to avoid: taking life; taking what is not given (do not steal); harmful sexual activity (such as adultery); telling lies; consuming alcohol and taking drugs. (6)

3   The first is that all conscious life is important and it is wrong deliberately to kill or harm it. Many Buddhists are therefore vegetarians. The second is we should not steal or take what is not ours. This includes not becoming rich at the expense of others. The third is we should not do sexually harmful things such as adultery. (6)

4   The first of the Five Precepts states that it is wrong to take life. This is because it is wrong to cause deliberate harm to any sentient being. Therefore many Buddhists are vegetarian because they argue that deliberately killing an animal when humans don't need to eat meat to stay healthy is wrong. (6)

5   A basic Buddhist teaching is that everything owes its existence to everything else. The world is not just here for human benefit but for all life. This means humans have a special role in maintaining the environment. They should show metta or loving kindness to all sentient beings and enable all things to live in harmony. (6)

8.12 Scriptures

1   The Buddhist scriptures are the teachings of the Buddha and the teachings of Buddhist scholars after his death. There are three baskets of scripture called the Tripitaka. The first is the Vinaya Pitaka – the rules for monks and nuns. The second is the Sutta Pitaka – the teachings of the Buddha. The third is the Abhidhamma Pitaka – philosophical teaching. (6)

2   Tripitaka means three baskets. Each basket contains different Buddhist scriptures. The first basket has rules for monks and nuns. The second contains the teaching of the Buddha called

the Dhammapada and the Jataka Tales. The third basket contains Buddhist philosophical teaching. (6)

3   If the person is bhikkhu or bhikkhuni then they will read and have read to them portions of the Vinaya Pitaka, which contain the rules for being a member of the monastic sangha. Lay people might recite the Dhammapada to help them meditate. The Jataka Tales might be used to teach children about the Buddha and his previous lives. (6)

4   In Japanese Zen Buddhism, a koan is a very popular form of teaching. A koan is a short saying, question or sentence that often seems to make little sense. A koan makes the person think about the meaning. A famous koan is 'What is the sound of one hand clapping?' (6)

5   The Jataka Tales are said to be about previous lives of the Buddha. They show the sort of lives a person should lead if he or she wants to become a buddha. Some are about people but many are about animals such as the Monkey King. Buddhists believe they have several lives before and after this one. (6)

9 Sikhism

9.1 Guru Nanak

1 He was born in Pakistan, the son of high caste Hindus, and he lived a good life. He was a religious man and one day, after praying, he felt God's presence. He started teaching people how to pray, live pure lives and give generously. In 1521 he founded the first Sikh community at Kartarpur and the first langar. He died in 1539. (6)

2 Guru Nanak was a great religious leader because he was intelligent and wise – this was noticed by his teachers even from an early age. He was also very modest and honest. He lived by the principles he taught. For example, he taught that Sikhs should be generous and he founded the free kitchen or langar. (6)

3 He began teaching people how to lead pure lives and how to pray and encouraged them to give generously to the poor. He went on four great teaching journeys to Hindu and Muslim holy places. He built a new town called Kartarpur where he and his disciples could work, learn and pray. He started a free kitchen for visitors. (6)

4 Guru Nanak spread his teaching by going on four long journeys all over India, Tibet, Iran and Iraq. He visited holy places and told people how to live a pure life. His friend Mardana was a musician and he used music to help people remember Nanak's teaching. Nanak taught his disciples in a Sikh community he founded in Kartarpur. (6)

5 Guru Nanak set his disciples a task. He asked them to carry a pile of muddy grass. While the others objected because they did not want to get dirty, Lehna carried it. Later they saw Guru Nanak drop a coin into a pool. Lehna retrieved it when the others refused. Guru Nanak therefore chose Lehna to be the next Guru. (6)

9.2 Guru Angad and Guru Gobind Rai

1 Guru Angad was appointed by Guru Nanak to be his successor. He was a man of humility and devotion, and he taught that people achieve salvation by being true to their duties. He also taught his disciples to be physically fit. He helped Sikhism to develop by collecting together Guru Nanak's hymns. (6)

2 Guru Gobind Rai was the last of the Ten Gurus. He led the Sikhs in their opposition to the emperor and restored their faith in God. He wrote poetry that gave his followers spiritual strength. In 1699 he chose five men who were prepared to give their heads for him to form the Panj Pyares. He was murdered in 1708. (6)

3 Guru Gobind Rai asked for volunteers to give their heads for him. One man volunteered and went into a tent. Gobind Rai returned with a blood-covered sword and asked for another volunteer. After four more men had volunteered in the same way, Gobind Rai led them all out alive and declared they were his beloved ones because they were prepared to die for him. (6)

4   The Khalsa began in Vaisakhi in 1699. Guru Gobind Rai asked for volunteers who would be prepared to die for him. Five men volunteered. One by one the men went into a tent with Gobind Rai, who then appeared with a bloody sword. Then the five men appeared unharmed. They had proved themselves fearless and faithful. They were called the Panj Pyares and became the basis of the Khalsa. (6)

5   Gobind Rai made the Sikhs strong by training them to be soldiers. He encouraged them to develop physical fitness and mental strength. His powerful poetry gave them spiritual strength and restored their faith in God. This inspired them and gave them confidence to fight their enemies. He also created the Khalsa, which gave Sikhs a sense of community. (6)

9.3 The Khalsa

1   The Khalsa is a group made up of the most dedicated Sikhs. It is a 'pure community' and the highest moral standards are expected. Members are willing to die for their faith and they adopt the name Singh, which means lion, or Kaur, which means princess. All members wear the five Ks. (6)

2   The five Ks are: kesh – uncut hair as a sign of God's gift; kangha – comb; kara – steel band, a sign that God is eternal; kachha – shorts, a sign of duties to others; kirpan – sword, a sign to protect the weak. (6)

3   Being a member of the Khalsa means living to high moral standards. A person's name reminds them of this. Singh means lion and describes how men are to be strong, caring and fearless. Kaur means princess and describes how women are to be treated like a princess by men. (6)

4   The kangha is a special comb that keeps men's long hair tidy. The kachha is a pair of under-shorts. They are worn as a sign of action and duty to others. The kirpan or sword is worn as a sign of freedom and to remind the wearer of his duty to protect the weak. (6)

5   The five Ks are important for members of the Khalsa because they remind them of their duties and beliefs. For example, uncut hair or kesh reminds them that their lives are a gift from God and that life is holy. The kirpan is a sign that the weak should be protected. Finally, the kara reminds them that only God is eternal. (6)

9.4 Guru Granth Sahib

1   Sikhs show respect to the Guru Granth Sahib by giving it the place of honour in the Gurdwara. People must sit below it and when it is moved everyone must stand up. It is wrapped in a clean embroidered cloth and a bearer carries it on his head. At home, it is often kept in a special room. (6)

2   The Guru Granth Sahib contains the teachings of the first five gurus. There are over 3000 hymns organised according to the tunes (or ragas) to which they are sung. At the beginning of the book are set prayers for morning, noon and evening. (6)

3   Sikhs treat the Guru Granth Sahib with great respect and use it to guide them in their daily lives. At home, Sikhs are expected to read right through it. They seek advice from it and it shows them how to have high moral standards. Reading from it is a central part of worship in the Gurdwara. (6)

4 The Guru Granth Sahib is important in two ways. Firstly, it is central to Sikh worship. In the gurdwara it is the central object of worship and is given place of honour. Without it, no ceremonies can take place. Secondly, it is believed to be the word of God, so its teaching is central to how a Sikh must behave. (6)

5 After the death of Guru Gobind Singh there were no more Gurus. The role of the guru was carried on by the Guru Granth Sahib. Its scriptures contain the teaching of the first five gurus. It was compiled by Guru Arjan, who also added his own teaching. (6)

9.5 Rahit Maryada

1 The Rahit is a code of conduct based on rules laid down for the Khalsa by Guru Gobind Singh. It says that true Sikhs should be honest, should give to the poor, should not steal or gamble and must do charitable work as well as their ordinary jobs. They should meet together and think about the gurbani. (6)

2 The Rahit Maryada contains the rules on how Sikhs should live their lives and think about the gurbani of the Guru Granth Sahib. It teaches that every family must pray before carrying out a task. It teaches that children should be educated and no one should drink alcohol or take drugs. Women should not wear veils. (6)

3 The Rahit came to be written down because over the years other rules were added to those that Guru Gobind Singh had laid down for the first Khalsa. These caused an argument so a special committee was set up to decide what rules to keep. The process took fifteen years but they were finally published in 1945. (6)

4 Sikhs should always behave honestly towards other people, both in business and at home. They should not steal. They should give to anyone who is hungry and offer help within the community. They should be in control of themselves and not drink alcohol or take drugs. (6)

5 The Rahit Maryada contains the rules on how Sikhs should live their lives and think about the gurbani of the Guru Granth Sahib. In the community, Sikhs should give money to help the poor and should not gamble and certainly never steal. It encourages people to become involved with community work and charities. (6)

9.6 Beliefs

1 Sikhs believe in reincarnation and their goal in life is to be free of it and to be one with God. If they lead bad lives where they are selfish or greedy or have wrong desires, they will be reborn. Guru Nanak said, 'One who seeks pleasure wanders from birth to birth not caring about God's will.' (6)

2 Sikhs believe that there is only one God and He is the creator and designer of the universe. He has no beginning and no end – nothing created Him. He is timeless. God's name is very important and it should be repeated often, by saying Waheguru. (6)

3 Sikhs believe that anyone who has lived a selfish life and ignored God's will is reincarnated. Once they have learned to live a good life following God's path by listening to the gurbani, they are released from this cycle of reincarnation. This state is called mukti and is given by God's grace. (6)

4   Mukti means being released from the cycle of rebirth to be united with God. It comes from the grace of God. Sikhs achieve mukti by listening to the gurbani, repeating the Name of God and meditating on it and through worship. Sikhs must be filled with God and then God might grant them mukti.   (6)

5   Sikhs listen to the gurus, who are their religious leaders. They must be upright people because their job is to lead people from darkness into light. They do this by telling them about the will of God for their lives and explaining the teaching in the Guru Granth Sahib.   (6)

9.7 Birth and initiation

1   The parents bring their baby to the front of the gurdwara where it is held above the Guru Granth Sahib. Special hymns of thanksgiving are sung and a name is chosen. Sometimes the baby's tongue is touched with a kirpan dipped in honey and water. The Ardas prayer is said and finally special food is distributed.   (6)

2   The baby is held above the Guru Granth Sahib and thanksgiving hymns are sung. The baby's name is chosen using the Guru Granth Sahib. The baby's tongue may be touched by a sword dipped in amrit. The Ardas prayer is said. Then Karah Parshad food is distributed. The parents may give a new cloth for the Guru Granth Sahib.   (6)

3   The baby's name is chosen from the Guru Granth Sahib. The book is opened at random. The baby's name has to begin with the first letter of the first word of the hymn on that page. The parents then decide on the name and it is announced to everyone.   (6)

4   Five full members of the Khalsa attend the ceremony. A reading is taken from the Guru Granth Sahib. Those being initiated are asked questions such as 'Do you believe in one God?' They receive the amrit five times and the Mul Mantra is said five times. The rules of Khalsa are explained and the Ardas is said.   (6)

5   The ceremony takes place when a person is about fifteen and wishes to become a member of the Khalsa. There must be five Khalsa Sikhs at the ceremony wearing the five Ks and saffron-coloured robes. The person reads from the Guru Granth Sahib and is asked various questions. The person then eats the amrit and the rules of the Khalsa are explained.   (6)

9.8 The gurdwara

1   People make offerings at the takht. Hymns are sung by special singers and then everyone meditates on the Name of God. They may listen to sermons on the teachings of the Gurus. Karah Parshad is placed by the Guru Granth Sahib and the Japji is said. Everyone faces the Guru Granth Sahib for a final reading and the final prayer.   (6)

2   The langar was first started by Guru Nanak and it makes sure people from different backgrounds and class all eat together. This is because in the eyes of God all people are created equal. It means that people in the community, especially the poor, are fed. It teaches people to give and be generous.   (6)

3   In a typical gurdwara you would see a large carpeted space with the palki at the end. In the middle of the palki is a raised cushion-covered platform where the Guru Granth Sahib rests. There is a canopy above it that is often decorated with gold and silver tinsel. This area is called the takht or throne.   (6)

4 The Nishan Sahib hangs outside a gurdwara. On it is a symbol of the Khalsa. It is a reminder of God's presence. Diwan consists of hymns sung by singers (ragi). The palki is a raised platform. The takht is the throne. The Guru Granth Sahib rests on the manji, which is a kind of stool and sits on the palki. (6)

5 Kirtan is the main part of worship and is the singing of hymns from the Guru Granth Sahib. The ragi do this and play musical instruments. While this happens everyone meditates on the name of God, which helps them achieve mukti. Karah Parshad is the holy sweet. Japji is the prayer offered when Karah Parshad is placed near the Guru Granth Sahib. (6)

9.9 Festivals

1 Vaisakhi is a festival celebrating the birth of the Khalsa. It was started by Guru Gobind Singh at a time of military training. Another festival is Diwali. It celebrates freedom and human rights because of Guru Hargobind. He enabled 52 Hindu princes to leave prison with him. There are firework displays and small oil lamps are lit. (6)

2 The Guru Granth Sahib is used in most Sikh festivals. Hymns are sung from it as in normal worship. At many festivals, the Guru Granth Sahib is processed. For example, it is carried ceremonially on the birthdays of Guru Nanak and Guru Gobind Singh, and at Vaisakhi. (6)

3 The Nishan Sahib always hangs outside a gurdwara or Sikh temple. On it is a symbol of the Khalsa. It is a reminder of God's presence. Therefore, when celebrating Vaisakhi, the Nishan Sahib is particularly significant as this festival celebrates the founding of the Khalsa. (6)

4 Vaisakhi remembers how the Khalsa was formed in 1699. The story of how Gobind Rai selected the first five members is told by pretending to cut off their heads. The festival marks the beginning of the Sikh New Year. Lots of games are played as signs of individual courage and team spirit. (6)

5 At Diwali Sikhs remember how Guru Hargobind left prison and returned to Amritsar and how 52 Hindu princes were freed at the same time by hanging onto his coat tails. There is worship in the gurdwara. There are firework displays and talks about Guru Hargobind's adventures. People light little oil lamps called divas and eat special meals. (6)

9.10 Marriage and death

1 In the gurdwara, the bride and groom sit opposite the takht. Their duties as husband and wife are read and then a blessing is said for them and their parents. The couple bows to the Guru Granth Sahib. They are given flowers and then they circle the Guru Granth Sahib four times. Often money is placed in their laps by guests. (6)

2 People go to the gurdwara to pay their last respects, then the body is taken to be cremated. Hymns are sung from the Guru Granth Sahib and the Ardas is said. The body is laid on the funeral pyre and then the funeral prayer is recited. The person's ashes can either be placed in flowing water or buried. (6)

3 Marriage is very important to Sikhs and they are strongly encouraged to get married. It is important because the love of the worshipper for God is likened to the love between husband and wife. Marriages are usually arranged but both parties have to agree or the marriage will not take place. (6)

4 Sikhs teach that Earth is not our permanent home and we should accept death as inevitable. The Guru Granth Sahib says, 'Each day that dawns must reach its end.' Sikhs believe that death either leads to reincarnation or to being one with God. Everyone is equal in death as no one can take physical strength or wealth with them. (6)

5 When someone is dying, the gurbani is read to them. After they have died, their body is washed and dressed in clean clothes and taken to the gurdwara. If the person is a Khalsa Sikh, the five Ks are worn. As the body is taken to the crematorium, hymns are sung and the Ardas is said. At the pyre, the evening prayer is recited. (6)

9.11 Places of pilgrimage

1 The Five Takhts refer to the five really important Sikh places of pilgrimage that have special authority and spiritual meaning. Guidance is offered under the leaders of the takhts and the Guru Granth Sahib. They are places where major religious decisions are made. The most important Takht is the Golden Temple at Amritsar. (6)

2 The Golden Temple is built in the centre of a bathing pool. Inside is a lot of black and white marble inlaid with precious stones. The temple is covered with sheets of gold. It is built of white stone and has doors all along its sides. There is a hall of mirrors to make it even more beautiful. (6)

3 There is a pool for worshippers to bathe in. The step down into the temple reminds Sikhs of the need for humility before God. The walls are decorated with writings from the Sikh scriptures. The ground floor contains the takht, palki and a rail to guide worshippers round the Guru Granth Sahib. The upper floor is for reading the Guru Granth Sahib. (6)

4 In front of the Golden Temple is a large pool. The building has many elaborate decorations and writings from the scriptures. As you enter the temple, you can see lots of black and white marble. On the ground floor is the takht and palki. On the second floor is a place for reading and a hall of mirrors. (6)

5 Worshippers must remove their shoes and wash their feet before entering. Heads must be covered. As they step down into the temple, they remember to be humble before God. They bow as they enter and as they walk round the Guru Granth Sahib they leave gifts inside the rail. As they leave they receive Karah Parshad. (6)